REFLE
FUNCTIONING
and Play

Strengthening attachment relationships in families from pregnancy to adolescence

Debi Maskell-Graham

First published 2016

Reprinted 2017 and 2020

big toes little toes
Registered with the Charity Commission for England and Wales

Registration No. 1152716

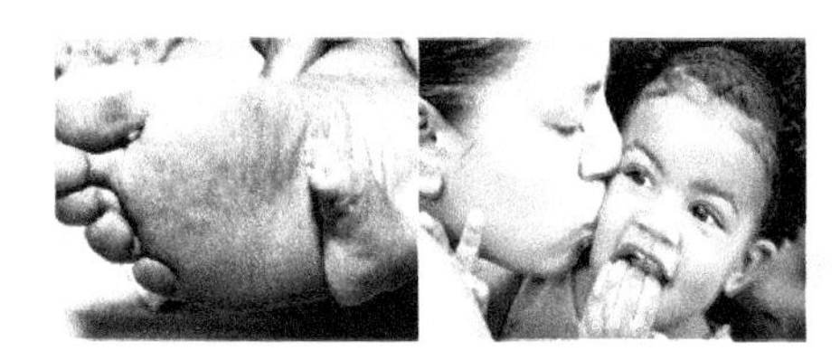

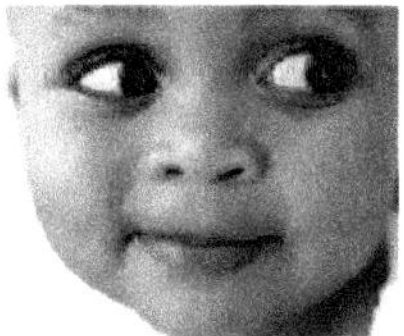

Images: iStock

Cover Design: Sophie Maskell

978-0-9957628-0-0

Printed in the UK

For my daughters, Sophie Emma and Chloe Annabel,

and my husband, Peter.

About the Author

Debi Maskell-Graham is Founder of big toes little toes, a charity registered in England and Wales. Over the last 30 years, she has been developing and facilitating innovative and strengths-based practice from within and alongside communities in the UK, and now around the globe. As a play therapist, researcher, trainer and consultant, she is passionate about translating attachment theory and the latest peer-reviewed research into playful, accessible and effective programmes to strengthen the parent–child relationship.

Acknowledgements

This book is the result of many years' experience of working with parents and carers and their children to support the earliest attachment relationship between them. It also comes from a passion to empower my fellow practitioners with practical, explicit and accessible attachment tools wherever they are around the globe. I wanted to articulate attachment mechanisms identified in the latest empirical research at practice level, and create a suite of programmes that would deliver positive relationship change on the ground – research delivered directly and explicitly into practice in ways not seen before.

I would like to thank the pilot "baby bonding" groups that took place in the UK from 2008. This early research and practice provided a strong foundation for me to build on. The lovely memories of parents and carers sharing, laughing and even crying together helped me to realise how vulnerable most parents feel when they have a baby. The work in the UK was followed by exciting developments in Africa and other parts of the world where the cross-cultural benefits of the approach were explored. Thank you to all of the parents and babies in Kisumu in Kenya and Cape Town in South Africa, and to Helen Howes and René Ohlhoff, who pioneered this early work.

This book builds on the research of many insightful scholars in the fields of infant mental health and Reflective Functioning and I would like to acknowledge their profound influence on my work. Of special note are Jane Barlow, John Oates, Dana Shai, Arietta Slade, Elizabeth Meins, Peter Fonagy, Michelle Sleed and Lynne Murray.

Finally, I would like to thank my lovely daughters and husband for their encouragement and patience as I have sought to break new ground. This book is for you.

Debi Maskell-Graham
May 2016

Contents

Table of Abbreviations

BMF	Behaviour, Meaning, Feeling (see p. 24)
HHH	Head, Heart and Hands (see p. 24)
MMM	Maternal Mind-Mindedness (see p. 19)
PDI	Parent Development Interview (see p. 19)
PEM	Parental Embodied Mentalising (see p. 20)
RF	Reflective Functioning
SDQ	Strengths and Difficulties Questionnaire (see p. 76)
TOPSE	Tool to measure Parenting Self Efficacy (see p. 77)

Notes to the reader

In order to allow the text to flow more easily, this book generally refers to parents, carers, children and practitioners as female.

The online resources bank are available via the website www.bigtoeslittletoes.org.

Introduction

> It was from words dropped little by little that everything was revealed to me.
>
> Antoine de Saint-Exupéry, *The Little Prince*

Being a 21st-century parent or carer is no easy task and yet it is the very thing we seem least prepared for when presented with a new addition to our families. It is not always clear what is best for us and our children with so many experts, blogs, books, TV programmes, friends and family offering advice. Who do we listen to?

Fortunately, the research community has already provided reliable findings telling us which children do best across all areas of life. This evidence tells us considerably more about the *types* of family relationships children thrive in rather than the best parenting styles or behavioural approaches. In other words, it is the *quality* of relationships between parents and children that makes the most difference. Focusing on family relationships rather than simply on parenting techniques or child behaviour might better reflect the weight of the research evidence.

Of course, parents and carers are very concerned with behaviour. Behaviour causes lots of trouble and worry for everyone, from children to parents, teachers to politicians, the police to the judiciary. Many parents and carers are worried that if the focus turns towards relational rather than behavioural strategies, they will somehow lose control and authority over their children. In fact, the opposite is true. If the key attachment relationships in children's lives are working, helpful behaviours and positive outcomes generally follow.

Babies, like all mammals, are designed to survive through keeping their parents and carers close by. They use "proximity-seeking" behaviour to make sure that they will be fed, watered and cared for. However, the nature of this behaviour is not decided by the baby. It is decided by the parent. In other words, babies come to learn what to expect from their parent and organise themselves around that. This is simply a matter of survival. Babies are very pragmatic.

So if a newborn baby is crying and dad comes fairly quickly to comfort her, she learns that the world is a safe and reliable place. If her experience is generally positive, she builds an expectation or internal "road map" that human relationships are reliable and predictable and meet her needs. She learns that she does not need to make a big fuss to get attention, or to keep quiet and not make any fuss because of unpleasant consequences. She takes this with her into future relational expectations and experiences.

Now imagine the baby crying for hours and no one coming to help her. Babies left to cry will stop eventually; essentially they give up. She has learned that no one comes to help and comfort her. Instead, she learns to soothe herself or shut down and numb such overwhelming feelings. The next morning she cries again. This time her mother comes immediately, picks her up, holds her tightly and bounces her up and down violently. Imagine that this situation is regularly extreme. This little one is confused and unable to work out what to expect from her close relationships. Her experiences of her mother are unpredictable: one minute high contact and overwhelming, the next, nothing at all. She cannot make a road map because it is overwhelming and disorganised, even frightening. She takes this disorganisation into her future relationships.

These scenarios represent the two extremes of attachment relationship. Which of the babies is likely to do better in life, be happier and healthier, able to make friends, learn and enjoy nursery and school, empathise with others – able to be all that she wants to be?

This book outlines a new suite of programmes across three developmental phases that is designed precisely to strengthen the parent–child attachment relationship. These programmes offer a theory-driven and evidence-based approach that can be adapted for a range of needs and contexts. Their main strength is the way in which they translate known attachment-generative mechanisms, identified in the research literature, into playful practical activity easily implemented by a range of practitioners.

To date, the programmes are active in the UK, Ireland, South Africa, Kenya, Uganda, Hong Kong, the Philippines, Singapore,

Thailand, Myanmar and India. Individual and group work is being used in schools, public-health clinics, hospitals, private clinics, adoption charities, fostering agencies, social-work agencies, farming communities, women's refuges and child-care settings, and in the community. Their playful and psycho-educational approach appears to translate very well across cultures and languages.

In Chapter 2 the scene is set with an overview of attachment and the challenges presented to researchers and practitioners by its apparent and puzzling intergenerational transmission.

Chapter 3 looks at the latest developments in research and thinking which go some way to deal with the problem of transmission gap. In particular, we can now identify a particular "state of mind" in a parent or carer that correlates with attachment security.

Chapter 4 examines why play is adopted as the means to strengthen attachment security in the parent–child relationship. A short overview of play theory allows us to be confident that a playful approach is both culturally and developmentally sensitive.

Chapter 5 introduces the suite of programmes and sets out their format and sessional structure. This structure translates, and makes operational, known attachment mechanisms into gentle, respectful and playful activity. Practical guidance is given on how to set up Reflective Functioning and play groups, one-to-one work and home visiting programmes. The chapter ends with the practitioner skills and qualities needed to deliver the programmes effectively. No book or manual can supersede the delivery skill of the practitioner.

Chapter 6 details resource materials to support programme delivery, including a series of sample six-week sessions – for babies, toddlers, children aged five to nine years and children and teens aged ten to fourteen years. Additional online resources are signposted, including a menu of activity ideas for each developmental stage, a practitioner community and a resources bank.

Chapter 7 outlines what to expect during programme delivery, including the developing group process. This is brought to life through two case studies. Common challenges are also addressed.

In Chapter 8 we examine the importance of measuring programme impact and suggest a suite of measures which may be useful to practitioners and those commissioning programmes. This chapter also signposts a number of programme evaluation studies and global case studies.

In the concluding chapter and epilogue, the focus is on the need for practitioners to take good care of themselves in order to maintain their physical and emotional capacity for undertaking this vital work. I also make a call for a society that is far more focused on understanding each other and on the everyday quality of our relationships. The respectful, reflective and playful skills outlined in this book would make for a very different society indeed and one in which I would much prefer to live.

All chapters conclude with a summary of headline messages. These are designed to highlight the most important points for readers.

As we now look at attachment theory and the tricky problem of its intergenerational transmission, I do hope that you enjoy the balance of theory, evidence and practice presented in this book. I believe that we need all three in order to be truly effective in this approach: the why, the what and the how.

Chapter 1 headline messages

The *quality* of parent–child relationships is more important than individual parenting styles

Babies need to keep their main carer (primary attachment figure) close by and will learn to adapt their behaviour accordingly

The strategies babies learn for maintaining proximity to their primary attachment figure will go on to become a dynamic "road map" or internal working model for future relationships

Babies who enjoy the optimal attachment relationship with their primary attachment figure are known to have the best outcomes across a wide range of domains and across their lifespans

Attachment and the transmission gap problem

> What is most important is invisible...
>
> Antoine de Saint-Exupéry, *The Little Prince*

Attachment theory, first put forward by John Bowlby in the 1960s, shows how babies form their expectations of relationships very early in life (Bowlby, 1969). His ideas are widely accepted across a range of fields including developmental, counselling and evolutionary psychology, ethology, neurobiology, epigenetics, psychology and psychotherapy. A crucial period, from around eight weeks after birth to around six to seven months, is known as "attachment-in-the-making". This is the period when babies are making sense (or not) of their key relationships and building their relational road map (Dozier, Manni and Lindheim, 2005). Bowlby calls this road map an internal working model (1969). It is possible to show that by the age of one babies have formed a dynamic internal working model of relationships by using The Strange Situation assessment protocol (Ainsworth et al., 1978; Goldberg, 2000). By this age, a baby's relationship with her parents and carers falls reliably into one of four attachment categories that define relationships along two interlinked domains: organisation and security.

Organised and secure

These babies receive "good enough" and responsive care from a very few consistent, loving and predictable main caregivers (known in attachment terms as primary attachment figures). From a North American and European perspective, we know that just over 60% of the general population enjoy at least one secure attachment with a primary attachment figure (Andreassen and West, 2007; van Izjendoorn et al., 1999). We also know that security of attachment only needs to be "good enough". In fact, Bornstein and Manian (2013) show that, as maternal responsiveness to the child increases, maternal sensitivity also increases to significance. However, after this point, where mothers' responsiveness becomes even more contingent, maternal sensitivity actually decreases. It seems that "some is better" rather than "more is better". Quoting Voltaire, the authors aptly note that the perfect is the enemy of the good. This should be a huge relief to many (guilt-ridden) parents!

Not only do securely-attached children flourish over their lifespans, but secure attachment has also been shown to be protective even in the face of considerable social and economic hardship (Cooper et al., 2009; WHO, 2004).

Insecure and anxious/resistant

These babies show excessive distress upon separation from their primary attachment figure, and when reunited tend to continue their distress. In other words, the baby is mis/distrustful of her primary attachment figure as a secure base. Features of this attachment style are insecurity, anxiety and dependency. Around 9% of the general population falls into this category (van Ijzendoorn et al., 1999). Whilst this category is not ideal, it is functional.

Insecure and avoidant

These babies have learned to suppress their natural desire to seek comfort from their primary attachment figure when frightened, distressed or in pain. In order to maintain physical proximity with their primary attachment figure, they "down-regulate". Making their needs known seems to drive their parents away or get a negative or unpleasant response. Around 15% of the general population are thought to fall into this category and, again, it is at least functional (ibid.).

Disorganised

This category was added later than the previous three when researchers identified a group of babies unable to organise themselves around their primary attachment figure at all (Main and Solomon, 1986; 1990). These children experience their parent in an unpredictable, overwhelming and often frightening/frightened way. It has been shown that around 15% of the general population fall into this category, which is also strongly associated with child abuse – physical, emotional and sexual – and child neglect (Carlson et al., 1989; van Ijzendoorn et al., 1999). These children have been shown to have poor outcomes and to be prone to poor mental health in adulthood (see, for example, Dozier et al., 1999; Fonagy et al., 1996; Ma, 2006). Where children have such challenging early relationship experiences in life, it is likely that they will need specialist intervention and support.

The research evidence is also clear on the kinds of futures or outcomes for different attachment relationships between parents and carers and children.

Babies who enjoy a secure attachment relationship with their primary attachment figure(s) do best on all outcome measures across their lifespan (Greenberg, 1999; Green and Goldwyn, 2002). It seems that early secure attachments set the scene for a generally happy and healthy life and for optimal success in social, educational, relational, psychological and economic spheres. Notably, secure attachment is related to children's social competence on school entry (Rispoli et al., 2013). Of course, other major life events and processes play their part but early attachment is consistently shown to impact on our children's life chances and can even predict the efficiency of neural regulation of positive affect 20 years later (Moutsiana et al., 2014).

Whilst secure attachment seems to offer a "buffer" against stress, early insecure-anxious/resistant attachment is linked with later anxiety and passive withdrawn behaviours (Greenberg, 1999; Weinfield et al., 1999). Early insecure-avoidant attachment has an association with later aggressive behaviours, anti-social behaviour and negative affect (Egeland and Carlson, 2004; Suess et al., 1992; Weinfield et al., 1999). Early insecure-disorganised attachment is strongly indicative of later hostility, aggression and dissociation (Egeland and Carlson, 2004; Greenberg, 1999).

There is also a worrying link between attachment problems and criminal behaviour. For example, Fonagy and Levinson (2004) found that, once psychiatric disorders had been controlled for, offenders were more likely to have attachment difficulties than the control group. In addition, the capacity of forensic patients to reflect on their own mental state or that of others was critically impaired and compromised their ability to empathise. This lack of empathy is important for reasons that will become clear later in this chapter when we discuss parental mind-state.

However, it is important to emphasise that attachment relationships and internal working models are dynamic and *can* be changed and remodelled (Pietromonaco and Barrett, 2000). Although the developmental window for the initial formation of the internal working model of attachment is from around eight weeks to six to seven months of age, all is not lost. However, the sooner parents and carers can be helped and supported to strengthen the quality of their relationships, the better. This is because it gets harder and harder to remodel unhealthy relationships. The process gets "tripped up" by the existing negative relationship patterns. Prevention is indeed better than cure.

The research community is united in its recommendation that relational support for parents ideally needs to begin in pregnancy and not just when the baby is born (Barlow, 2016). Pregnancy is, in fact, the ideal moment to support parents and represents "a window of opportunity" (Brandon et al., 2009; Rackett and Holmes, 2010).

Attachment across family generations

Attachment research also tells us how attachment relationships operate across families. In the late 1990s, researchers began to realise that attachment patterns in families appeared to be passed down from one generation to the next (De Wolff and van Ijzendoorn, 1997). This became known as the intergenerational transmission of attachment. Studies began to explore this phenomenon more closely (see, for example, O'Connor and Croft, 2001; Ravel et al., 2001). Evidence could link sensitive and loving parents and carers with securely attached children but the relative impact of these known factors was small (De Wolff and van Ijzendoorn, 1997). In other words, there were other things going on in family relationship patterns linked to secure attachment. There was a gap in the knowledge that became known as the transmission gap.

This gap also raises a difficult idea, that loving parents are not the whole story and that love in itself is not enough for secure attachment. This seems a tough message, but then even abusive parents say that they love their children. Maybe love is not enough?

The transmission gap and Reflective Functioning

Over the next twenty years, researchers began to identify a specific skill or capacity in parents that was linked directly to the quality of their relationships with their children (Fonagy and Target, 1997; Slade, 2005). It was something much more specific than love –

which is arguably hard to define. Potentially, researchers had found something to at least partially address the problem of transmission gap.

Researchers identified that parents whose children were securely attached had a specific ability or orientation (Grienenberger et al., 2005). They acknowledged and accepted the infant as a separate and emerging psychological agent with her own mind. They could focus on and think about their children, see the world from their point of view, and make them feel understood. These parents were trying hard to understand and respond to their children and in return children were responding positively. It sounds a little like empathy but actually goes further, because it demands that parents and carers understand their own mental states in relation to their children's and the complexities of the interactions between them (Allen et al., 2008; Choi-Kain and Gunderson, 2008). Attachment researchers called it Reflective Functioning (hereafter generally referred to as RF). They also discovered that parents could get better at it with help and practice. It seemed to operate on a sliding scale, with sufficiency yielding positive attachment change in the parent–child relationship (Slade, 2006).

A range of intervention trials followed, mainly aimed at parents with highly complex needs, for example those with drug and alcohol issues (Pajulo et al., 2006, 2012; Sadler et al., 2006; Suchman et al., 2010) and those suffering from past trauma and domestic violence (Kearney and Cushing, 2012; Schechter et al., 2006; Stern, 2014). The results were encouraging and established a robust link between good-enough levels of parental RF and secure attachment relationships between children and parents.

A Reflective Functioning programme to bridge the transmission gap problem

During my postgraduate research at Canterbury Christ Church University and at the Warwick Infant and Family Wellbeing Unit at Warwick Medical School, I became very interested in RF. It appeared to be a capacity or skill that could grow and improve. Maybe it could even be learned. I was keen to explore if it could be translated into a playful and practical approach for parents and carers and children around the globe. I saw a need for *all* families to benefit from knowing about attachment mechanisms and introducing them into everyday family life.

I conducted a Realist synthesis (Pawson and Tilley, 1997) of more than 140 peer-reviewed papers, up to and including early 2016, relating to theory and intervention focused on improving RF in parents. Bringing the findings together, I began to identify what these studies could reveal about the change mechanisms present in effective RF interventions. What could these studies tell us about what works, for whom, in what respects, to what extent, in what contexts, and how? Moreover, was there a consensus on the underlying generative mechanisms that needed to be present in an intervention to yield improvements in parental RF capacity?

The synthesis of these findings showed RF as the primary change mechanism and active ingredient in effective interventions. However, there were other shared elements in these studies. A successful RF intervention had a set of secondary mechanisms that acted as a support to increasing RF capacity in parents and carers.

A detailed understanding of the primary and secondary generative mechanisms led to the creation of the programmes presented in this book and split into three developmental phases:

1. Late pregnancy and the early months after birth – the perinatal period ("baby bonding")
2. Toddlerhood and the early years ("toddler bonding")
3. School-aged children and teenagers ("heart-to-heart").

Before we look further at the programme structure and content, it is important to take a detailed look at RF, its role in attachment and how it is made operational in the parent–child relationship.

Chapter 2 headline messages

A crucial period in the development of attachment is from around eight weeks after birth to six to seven months ("attachment-in-the-making")

As babies make sense of their experiences of their main caregiver (primary attachment figure), they form a dynamic internal working model of attachment

Babies can be shown to fall into four attachment categories or types along two domains (organisation and security): organised and secure; organised and insecure (anxious/resistant); organised and insecure (avoidant); and disorganised

Approximately 60% of a normative population enjoys an organised and secure attachment

A secure attachment is linked to optimal outcomes for children across their lifespans

A secure attachment offers a "buffer" against stress and is protective even in the face of hardship and deprivation

The intergenerational transmission of attachment has been identified but only recently have its mechanisms been understood. One such mechanism is RF

RF is a parental skill and/or capacity which appears to operate on a sliding scale. Adequate parental RF is linked with secure attachments in children

Any intervention seeking to nurture or improve parental RF also needs a set of secondary mechanisms in place which act to support its development

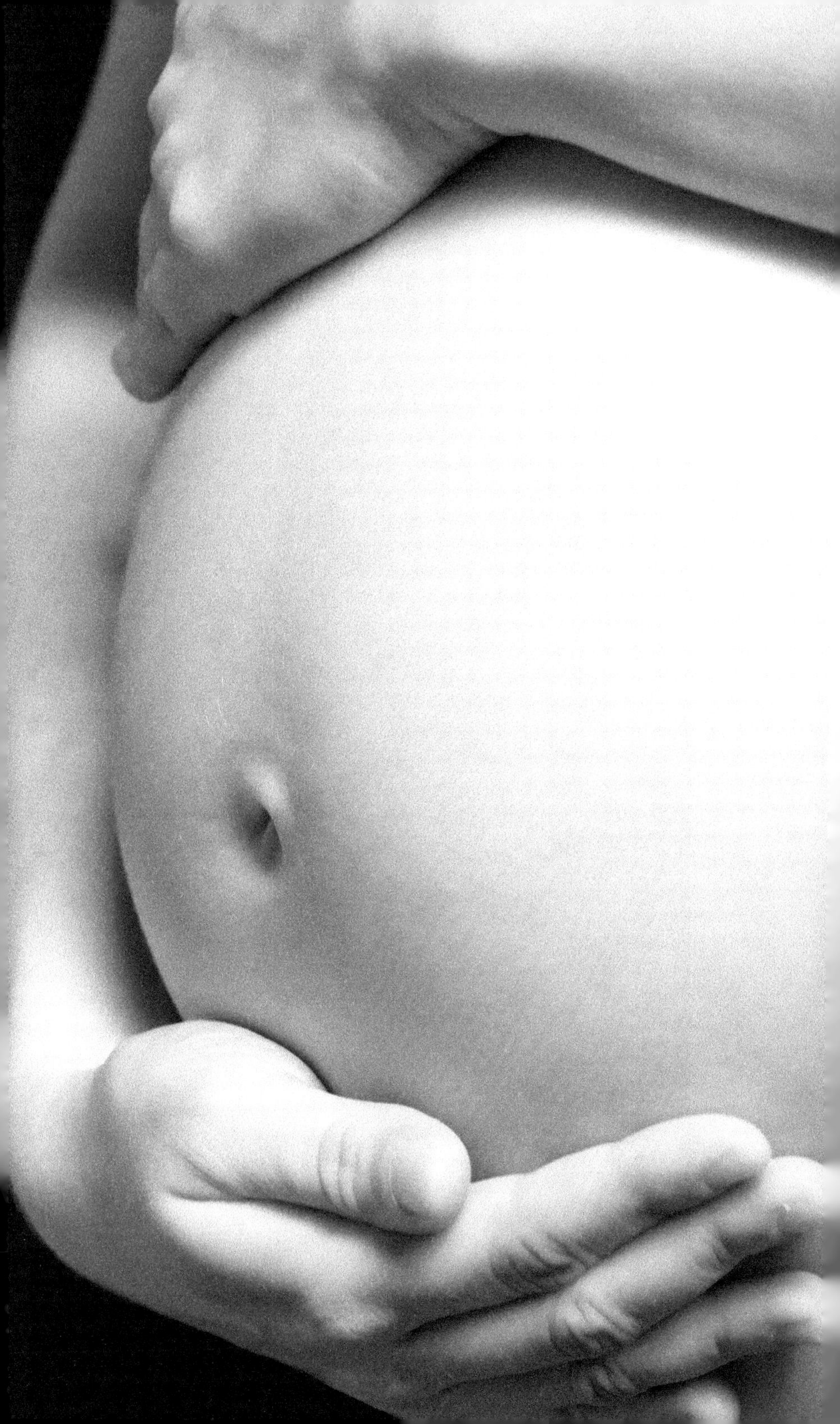

Infant psychological agency and Reflective Functioning

> This water was indeed a different thing from ordinary nourishment. Its sweetness was born of the walk under the stars, the song of the pulley, the effort of my arms. It was good for the heart, like a present.
>
> Antoine de Saint-Exupéry, *The Little Prince*

As we have seen in the previous chapter, recent research has identified a key parental capacity or ability that partly explains how attachment is made operational in early parent–infant relationships (Slade et al., 2005). In other words, researchers have moved beyond describing parental caregiving qualities such as sensitivity and warmth as indicators of security of attachment. We can now identify (and measure) an underpinning "state of mind" in the parent or carer towards their child. This is very exciting. If there is an identifiable parental skill or capacity associated with secure attachment, then it might well be possible to nurture, increase or even teach it.

The term "Reflective Functioning" was first coined by Peter Fonagy and colleagues and is the ability to imagine mental states in ourselves and others (Fonagy and Target, 1997). Through this capacity for reflection, we come to understand our own behaviour and responses, the behaviour and responses of others, and how these interact and intertwine. Essentially, we begin to make meaning out of our own and others' inner mental states. Fonagy and colleagues describe it as our uniquely human capacity to make sense of each other (Fonagy et al., 2004).

Numerous researchers have studied how RF operates in the relationship between parent and child. A parent with high RF can see her child as a separate and autonomous being with "a mind of her own." The child has her own thoughts, feelings, desires and intentions, which the parent recognises. Vitally, this parent also recognises that her own thoughts, feelings, desires and intentions are in interplay with the child's. An adequate RF ability in the parent has been shown to strengthen the parent–child relationship (see, for example, Katznelson, 2014). It has also been shown to help children to understand and regulate their behaviour leading to better self-control. In addition, parental RF is related to improved social competence, school-readiness and cognitive abilities in children (Belsky et al., 1991; Berlin and Cassidy, 2003; Rispoli et al., 2013).

In turn, RF rests on parental acceptance of their baby as a unique individual with her own mind and sense of self. As such, the baby is recognised as a distinct psychological agent. Infant psychological agency is a relatively recent research area. A reflective psychological agent can be defined as an autonomous system able to think about both one's own and others' explicit intentions and beliefs, and how these play out (Baron-Cohen, Tager-Flusberg and Cohen, 1993).

As technology has improved, developmental psychologists have been able to explore and identify different and sequential stages of psychological agency in very young children (see, for example, Gopnik, 2009). One key finding is that the infant's emerging psychological agency may only be able to develop in the presence of other similar and agentive minds, most notably the mind of the parent or carer (Stern, 1985).

In this respect, the infant's mind and self is separate from but inextricably linked to her experiences – good and bad – of the primary attachment figure's own mind and intentional self. Importantly, these early experiences are mediated through feeling states (Sharp and Fonagy, 2008) and this does not always go well.

This model of early psychological agency and the stages of its development have challenged the long-held view that we all somehow know our own minds and how we feel and think about things (Gopnik, 1993). In fact, the only way we can come to know our own thoughts and feelings is in the presence of another reflective mind – the mind of our primary attachment figure.

The assumption that the mind somehow knows itself masks the distinction between two aspects of the development of the self: the categorical and the subjective. The categorical self (Harter, 1999) is an individual's understanding of himself or herself based on other people's reactions to him or her; for example, being seen as attractive, sociable or intelligent or not, or "good" or "bad" at various skills and activities; accepted truths gained from others' views and opinions – an "outside–in" process.

The subjective self, however, is developed through an introspective and reflective ability to know one's own thoughts and feelings as distinct from the thoughts and feelings of others. This enables a true and unique sense of self to develop – an "inside–out" process.

Historically, it was assumed that all individuals were able to reflect upon their own and others' mind states and connected behaviours – the more so to understand the differences between their own and others' thoughts and feelings and the complicated interplay between them. However, it has become clear that this ability can be limited or even absent and its development in an individual depends upon a number of relational and social factors. This is very important because the absence or impairment of the subjective self is associated with mild to severe psychopathology (Fonagy et al., 2004).

If the baby's capacity to develop a subjective sense of self is not given but built in the presence of "more mature minds … both benign and reflective in their turn" (ibid., p.4), it follows that parental caregiving will generally need to embody these characteristics if the infant is to develop psychological agency. It seems that babies need to bask and grow in the presence of benign and reflective parental minds.

As we have already seen, RF is the individual's capacity to be aware of and reflect on his or her own mental state and that of others, and how these mental states are in interplay and translated into behaviour. It enables adaptive mentalisation processes to occur, but RF also has a protective function. The development of a secure attachment occurs in those infants whose parents are either securely attached themselves or have *enough* RF capacity for their own insecure patterns and behaviours to be successfully recognised and mediated (Slade et al., 2005).

Pregnancy offers a unique opportunity to support the early development of RF in expectant parents and thus promote the attachment relationship between mother and infant (Pajulo et al., 2006). During pregnancy, maternal representations are activated through representations of the baby, early motherhood and the maternal role. This can be a difficult period for those mothers who themselves have distorted, negative or idealised representations of their own childhood and subsequently their own parenting capacity. The ways in which the parent reflects on her own experience as a parent and on her child's mental states and experiences regulate, fail to regulate or even dysregulate the child's internal world (Grienenberger et al., 2005). RF seems to be a critical factor, with a number of studies showing that mothers who can reflect on their own experiences of childhood and parenting, regardless of the quality of these, are most likely to have securely attached infants (Fonagy et al., 1991; Pajulo et al., 2006).

This is exciting news for practitioners, who could provide a critical role in nurturing RF sufficiency in parents and carers whose own attachment experiences have been compromised or impaired.

For attachment theorists, the concept of RF is far-reaching in terms of setting the scene for a range of longer-term childhood outcomes. Not only do the infant's early caregiving experiences establish and potentially alter her mind, but they also affect her ongoing ability to function as a psychological agent (Main, 1994). Thus, RF functions as a process by which attachment security is passed on from parent to child. This addresses the Transmission Gap problem noted in Chapter 2.

Secure attachment results in part from accurate and appropriate parental mentalising of the child, which in turn positively stimulates the development of the mentalising capacity in the child. In turn, the mentalising child is able to form a secure attachment to the parent (Fonagy and Target, 1997). If this child goes on to become a parent, she takes her mentalising capacity into the next generation, and so on. It is easy to see how this can go wrong, with serious ongoing consequences for families.

The child's earliest mentalising capacity is developed through a social biofeedback model of affect-mirroring or marked mirroring (Fonagy et al., 2004). Thus, a primary attachment figure responds to their baby's emotional displays with appropriate displays of their own. In particular, the primary attachment figure "marks" their own response in ways that help the baby make sense of their original feelings. This marked mirroring can be seen happening between parents and babies in many everyday experiences. For example, the mum who responds to her unhappy baby's cries by pulling her own sad face and saying "What's the matter, little one? Not happy, eh?"; or the dad trying to feed his frowning and tight-lipped toddler: the dad also frowns, tilts his head and purses his lips in a slightly

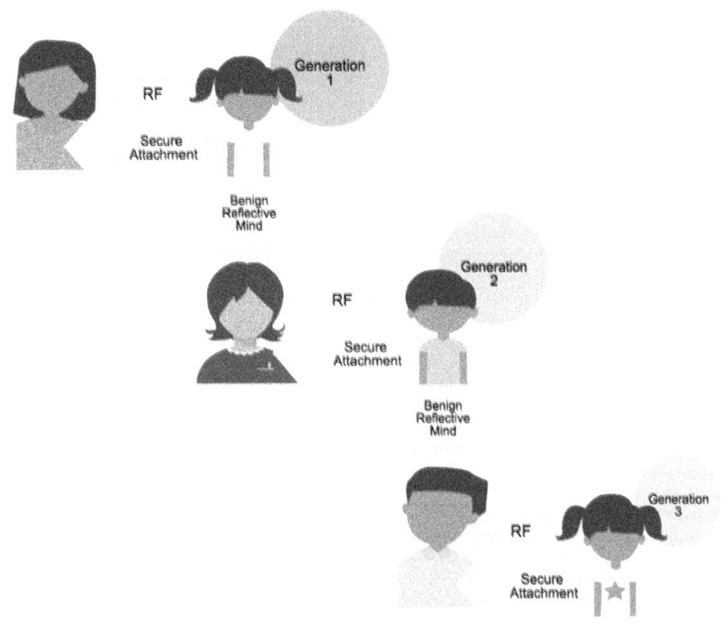

Figure 3.1: RF and the intergenerational transmission of attachment

exaggerated way, and says "You're not going to let this spoon in there, are you?"

Slade and colleagues (Grienenberger et al., 2005; Slade et al., 2005; Slade, 2005) expanded the concept of parental mentalising to explain the parental capacity not only to recognise mental states but also to link mental states to behaviour in meaningful and accurate ways. They also extended the use of the construct of RF to parental narratives about their relationships with their own children. They could identify RF in the ways in which parents and carers talked about their child and their child's thoughts, feelings and behaviours.

This led to the development of the Parent Development Interview (PDI) (Aber et al., 1985; Slade et al., 2002, 2005) designed to capture and measure parental RF capacity in the context of their current and ongoing relationship with their child. The PDI is a "gold standard" measure in terms of assessing parental RF.

Along with RF, another body of research was articulating a specific parental capacity to treat the child as a psychological agent known as Maternal Mind-Mindedness (MMM) (Meins et al., 2001). An emergent type of parental talk or narrative was identified that showed the parent's ability to hold the infant in mind. Across a number of studies, Meins and her colleagues showed that the children of mothers who were mind-minded and who treated their children as individuals with their own minds and intentions were more likely to be securely attached (Arnott and Meins, 2007; Laranjo et al., 2008; Meins et al., 2001; 2002; 2003; 2012). MMM is evidenced through a type of talk that acknowledges that the infant is able to have intentions and desires. Moreover, Meins argues that it is a maternal capacity to treat the infant as a mental agent that shows an understanding of the infant's ability to form representations of her experiences.

Both RF and MMM have drawn research attention to a type of parental discourse that evidences a mentalising capacity. As we have seen, adequate functioning in this type of parental talk is associated with secure attachment. However, there is debate over both the purpose and the function of this form of talk (see, for example, Shai and Belsky, 2011). Indeed, the mentalising talk could be evidence of parental RF capacity. In this respect, it could be said that non-verbal RF is the primary capacity and verbal RF the secondary.

As a consequence of this, a non-verbal measure of RF capacity has recently been developed, called Parental Embodied Mentalising (PEM) (Shai, 2010). PEM uses a non-verbal and whole-body (kinaesthetic) mode of parental mentalising. This can be seen (and measured) as the parent's capacity to implicitly understand the infant's mental state from the infant's whole-body expressions and to respond to these through the parent's own kinaesthetic expressions. This approach emphasises the importance of non-verbal communication (Shai and Belsky, 2011).

This growing understanding of RF as both a verbal and non-verbal capacity or skill has been explicitly woven into the suite of programmes outlined in this book. We need to explicitly seek to nurture, expand, foster, support and essentially grow RF in its verbal and non-verbal forms. However, in itself, even this is not enough. These programmes also need to address and reduce the risk factors known to impede its growth. In particular, parents and carers need to be helped to process, regulate and moderate their own highly aroused and potentially distorted affective states and reactions activated in them by their babies and children.

We will now look at the evidence base to date and see that, along with the positive nurturance of RF, programmes have also sought to reduce the risk factors which threaten its growth.

Reflective Functioning interventions: the evidence

A number of parenting interventions have been designed and tested which support early secure attachment relationships through the explicit development and nurturance of RF capacity as either a primary or secondary aim.

Many of the early infant mental health treatments focus primarily on changing parental internal working models (Tomlin et al., 2009). For example, Fraiberg's Parent–Infant Psychotherapy (Fraiberg, Adelson and Shapiro, 1975) focuses on improving parental behaviour by changing mental representations. "Watch, Wait and Wonder" (Cohen et al., 1999) involves the parent following the child's lead in ways that promote and nurture parental sensitivity and responsiveness. Interaction Guidance (McDonough, 2004) enables parents to conceptualise their loving care of their baby as a reflection of the representational world of the caregiver and infant.

In keeping with increased understanding about the link between attachment and RF, more recent intervention models have had a more direct and explicit focus on increasing parental RF as a primary aim.

The Yale Child Study Center has developed two RF parenting programmes, the first a group intervention for low-risk parents and children (Parents First) and the second a home visiting programme for high-risk parents and children (Minding the Baby).

Parents First was conceived as a preventative intervention to be delivered within normal educational and childcare settings. At its core is the importance of supporting children's cognitive and socio-emotional development from within the context of the parent–child relationship (Slade, 2006). The programme consists of 12 voluntary workshops aimed at enhancing parental RF though a number of activities including a series of reflective exercises.

The Minding the Baby programme (Sadler, Slade and Mayes, 2006) showed positive improvements in parental RF in traumatised teenage parents by fostering an ability in the parent to hold their baby "in mind" in many ways. This intervention involves a multidisciplinary approach and home visits from a team including a paediatric nurse and social worker, who work with the parent to help her to think about the baby's possible intentions and feeling states. Results showed improved health, mental health and socio-emotional outcomes, including an increase in maternal RF as measured by the PDI (Aber et al., 1995; Slade et al., 2005).

A Finnish intervention programme, Holding Tight, is based on the Minding the Baby approach and focuses on parents with problems of alcohol and substance misuse (Pajulo et al., 2012; Söderström and Skårderud, 2009). Through a mentalisation-based approach beginning in pregnancy, high-risk mothers are encouraged to invest in their babies instead of substances. Pajulo and colleagues (2012) show that, in a study of 34 mother-and-infant pairs – admitted to this intensive residential programme either during pregnancy or within two weeks of the infant's birth – pre-intervention RF scores were variable across the sample. However, these scores increased significantly over the life of the intervention, which lasted a minimum of four months. The researchers conclude that an intervention beginning in pregnancy that supports the mother's RF abilities in addition to encouraging abstinence is likely to have a significant effect.

The New Beginnings programme for mothers and babies in prison is an attachment-based group intervention (Baradon et al., 2008). A recent cluster randomised control trial examined outcomes for 88 mothers and babies participating in the New Beginnings programme and 75 dyads who resided in non-participating prisons. Outcomes were measured in terms of RF capacity, the quality of mother–infant interactions, maternal depression and maternal representations of their babies. Mothers in the control group showed a deterioration in both RF and the quality of interaction with their babies over the life of the study, whereas the intervention group showed no deterioration. Self-reported measures of depression and maternal representations of their babies showed no significant group effects (Sleed, Baradon and Fonagy, 2013). Interestingly, RF capacity was only maintained rather than improved in the intervention group.

The Family Minds psycho-educational and interactive programme is a recent development in RF intervention targeting foster and adoptive parents (Bammens, Atkins and Badger, 2015). It comprises elements of mentalisation-based family therapy, presentations, group exercises and home-based activities and lasts for a total of nine hours. The treatment group showed significant increased RF in comparison to a control group who received the usual treatment.

Another Finnish programme, Families First, is a group programme based on the Parents First programme originally developed at the

Yale Child Study Center (Kalland et al., 2016). Targeting the whole family, Families First aims to enhance parental mentalisation capacity and sensitivity in parent–child interaction. Interestingly, it targets first-time parents with no identified risk in order to protect the future relationship from adversity (a health promotion approach). Delivered within universal services by non-therapeutic staff, it aims to reach a large proportion of the population with minimal drain on specialist healthcare services. Lasting for 12 weeks, this group approach is currently underway, with data collection continuing until the end of 2016.

In summary, intervention studies to date have been able to show a correlation between RF and attachment. Importantly, they also show us a range of stressors/supports or risk/protective factors that influence intervention outcomes. It is a clear understanding and implementation of the primary and secondary mechanisms that will strengthen attachment relationships and empower parents and carers.

We now go on to look at how we present the idea of RF to parents and carers and build-in the known supports needed to mediate the factors that may impede its growth and development.

Presenting Reflective Functioning to parents and carers

The programmes in this book centre on a family-friendly way of describing, learning and practising RF as the core mechanism of the approach. This comprises two stages:

1. Bringing RF into parental consciousness and awareness
2. Guiding the development of parental RF capacity through a series of clear stages

Bringing RF into parental consciousness and awareness

To bring RF into the minds and hearts of parents and carers, the concept and its importance to attachment security is introduced to parents at the beginning of each programme.

An accessible metaphor is used to explain that RF manifests in three ways which are interlinked and in interplay; through thoughts (Head), feelings (Heart) and actions (Hands). Head, Heart and Hands (HHH) is shared with parents and carers to enable them to be more conscious and aware of RF in their day-to-day interactions with their children.

Head, Heart and Hands (HHH)

HEAD: us as parents focusing on our child and thinking about her and her thoughts – seeing the world through her eyes and from her point of view and understanding that her thoughts, ideas and intentions are separate from ours; us as parents knowing and recognising that our own thoughts can be affected by our child's thoughts and vice versa in complicated and sometimes painful ways.

HEART: us as parents putting ourselves inside our child and feeling her feelings – feeling what it is like for her – realising that her feelings are separate from ours; recognising our own feelings and responses to our child; knowing that our child's feelings can affect our feelings and vice versa in complicated and sometimes painful ways.

HANDS: in response to thinking and feeling, us as parents doing and saying things to let our child know that we are trying to understand her – acknowledging that her individual thoughts and feelings are respected as separate from ours (guessing is good, because it is very hard to mind-read!); understanding that our thoughts and feelings affect our children's thoughts and feelings and the quality of our interactions with them, again in complicated and sometimes painful ways.

A second technique is also used, especially where parents and carers find HHH a little too conceptual and need to begin with observing concrete behaviours. This guided observation questioning technique is known as Behaviour, Meaning, Feeling (BMF).

Behaviour, Meaning, Feeling (BMF)

BEHAVIOUR: Let's really watch our little one and notice every tiny thing she does – breathing, twitching, blinking, flicking of fingers, a hiccup – just keep watching moment-to-moment

MEANING: What does this behaviour mean? What is behind it?

FEELING: What feeling is this behaviour trying to communicate?

Along with these practice techniques, further information on RF is given as appropriate, including accessible research findings. When parents and carers are equipped with this knowledge, they can go some way to practising RF consciously.

Guiding the development of parental RF through a series of clear stages

Knowing about RF is not sufficient to facilitate its nurturance and growth. Thus, a series of progressive stages is built into the programmes that support and "scaffold" the development of parental RF. These stages are based on those developed by the team at Yale Child Study Center (Slade, 2006).

Sequential stages of RF development	
Stage 1: Developing a reflective stance	Practitioner models a reflective stance in ways which are non-threatening to parents and carers, for example through giving a voice to their child's mental states and through the use of their own "baby" (baby massage doll or teddy)
Stage 2: Facilitating wondering	Supporting parents and carers to take time to watch their child and wonder about their thoughts and feelings. Helping parents to move from accurately describing children's behaviours to guessing about their intentions, desires and feelings. For example, the practitioner starts with "what is she doing?" "I wonder why she's doing that?" "What does it mean?"
Stage 3: Eliciting affect	Gently helping parents and carers cope with strong feelings and emotions (which are often dysregulating for parents) and use them as a platform for reflection
Stage 4: Holding the parent in mind	Helping parents and carers to regulate their own distress in response to their children through the security of the relationship with the practitioner

Known secondary supports needed to promote parental RF

Additional core supportive elements, which are fundamental to the success of an intervention based on RF, are built into the programmes. These are the secondary generative mechanisms identified in the RF literature and are shown along with the primary mechanism (RF) in Figure 3.2 below.

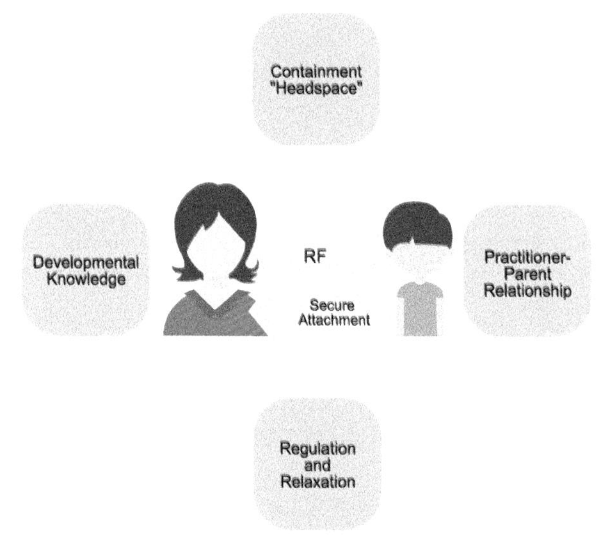

Figure 3.2: Primary and secondary generative mechanisms

Respectful and authentic practitioner–parent relationships

Trusting, supportive and non-judgemental relationships between parents, carers and practitioners are fundamental. It is the *quality* of the relationship between families and professionals that sets the scene for parents to develop their RF skills. In other words, parents thrive on consistent practitioner help that is reflective, respectful and honest. Parents and carers need time to be heard, and do best with reliable and predictable professional relationships built up over time.

In addition, the importance of the practitioner–parent relationship acknowledges the profound influence of the Transmission

Gap problem commonly present in many families regardless of background. Many parents have not experienced being raised in the presence of a "benign and reflective" mind. The programme practitioner must stand in the gap for parents and carers and offer them a space to enjoy this for themselves even as we ask them to offer this to their child(ren).

Containment (or "headspace")

Parents' and carers' worries and concerns take up thinking space in their heads. Where parents are worried or preoccupied by their day-to-day problems – for example, housing or food poverty – this reduces their capacity to develop RF. Any help offered to parents needs to include a containing space and practitioners who can contain and settle everyday worries and anxieties. Those commissioning programmes also need to think about how to build support networks for families that go beyond a short-term or ad hoc programme approach.

In addition, helpful and practical signposting to other support services needs to be in place, as this can also reduce the burden on parental headspace.

Developmental knowledge

Parents and carers who understand the physical, emotional, social and neurological development of their child are more able to develop and use their RF skills. They understand the norms for each stage and tend to have realistic expectations of what their child can and cannot do. Developmental knowledge empowers parents and helps them to see the "whole" child rather than just their behaviours. Parents and carers enjoy becoming the experts in their child's overall development and this needs to be actively and explicitly encouraged.

As mentioned earlier, parents and carers also benefit from *explicit* exploration and understanding of the role of RF in attachment security. Combining psycho-educational and creative activities helps parents and carers to become reflective about RF itself and more conscious of its internal operation within them. This happens even if RF is compromised by difficult feelings within the parent or carer.

Regulation and relaxation

Parents and carers who are gently helped to recognise, reflect on and manage their own difficult and overwhelming feelings in response to their children are more able to use their RF skills. It is essential, then, to offer reflective regulatory and relaxation opportunities and techniques to parents and carers.

The programmes outlined in this book offer creative ideas to nurture parents and help them increase their ability to contain themselves. We encourage parents to be "bigger" and "kinder" and encourage them as they discover internal resources which help them to be predictable, calm and contained with and for their child(ren).

This chapter has outlined the essential components of an effective RF programme including a parent-friendly way of presenting the concept, the sequential stages of the development of RF capacity and the supports needed to promote its growth. Altogether, these represent the active mechanisms operationalising attachment in the parent–child relationship.

However, we still need a delivery method or modality to provide the context for these mechanisms to flourish. We will now go on to look at why we use everyday play and playful creative activity as the means to deliver the programme mechanisms.

Chapter 3 headline messages

Adequate parental RF is associated with security of attachment in children

RF is a skill and/or capacity which enables the parent to see their child as an autonomous being with her own thoughts, feelings, desires and intentions

This parent also recognises that her own thoughts, feelings, desires and intentions are in interplay with her child's, sometimes in complicated and painful ways

Practitioners can play a crucial role in nurturing parental RF capacity and sufficiency

RF is one of the ways in which the intergenerational transmission of attachment is operationalised

Effective RF interventions nurture parental RF as a primary aim and address the risk factors that impede its growth

The successful development of RF in parents and carers comprises two stages: bringing RF into parental consciousness and awareness; and guiding the development of parental RF through a series of clear stages

Educating parents and carers *about* RF is not enough

Why use play to strengthen attachment?

> And no grown-up will ever understand that this is a matter of so much importance!
>
> Antoine de Saint-Exupéry, *The Little Prince*

In this book, everyday and creative play is the means through which RF is learned and practised by parents and enjoyed by children.

Why use play? Play is widely regarded in the literature as a spontaneous and active process and one in which "thinking, feeling and doing" creatively flourish (Bruce, 2011). Play is not shackled by reality and provides a deeply satisfying means for children to take charge of their own world where the usual dangers, rules and worries do not have to apply.

Play theory tells us many things about the nature and benefits of children's play. Through play, children enjoy exploring their world, testing out and trying new things or ways of being; they learn and practise many social skills; develop a sense of who they are; learn to interact with others, how to make friends, how to distinguish between truth and lies and how to role-play and try out other identities and roles. Importantly, they also learn how to experiment, to fail and to keep on trying (see, for example, Sutton-Smith, 1997; Lester and Russell, 2008).

But most of all play is essential purely for playing's sake. It is a complex yet instantaneous process, deeply enjoyable and sometimes risky, and enriches children's lives in multiple ways. Research shows children need freedom, space and time to play. Indeed, children's right to play is enshrined in Article 31 of the United Nations Convention of the Rights of the Child (UNICEF, 1991), emphasised by a General Comment stating that "play and recreation are essential to the health and well-being of children ..." (UNCRC, 2013).

Play is also pivotal in helping children regulate and process emotional responses to events and disturbance. It can reduce children's stress levels and help them process difficult feelings and experiences in the safety and metaphors created by imagination. It can also improve physical ability and development. Whilst playing, children are required to be curious and observant, to ask and respond to questions and problems. They make choices and develop their imagination, creativity and ways of thinking.

Conversely, the literature on play draws interesting conclusions on the harmful effects of play deprivation (Brown and Webb, 2005). For example, the White Rose Initiative took play workers into a Romanian paediatric hospital in the early 1990s following the overthrow of Ceausescu. Their work was able to mitigate the extreme effects of neglect experienced by institutionalised children through everyday play (ibid.). Prior to the project, the children – aged between one and ten years – had suffered chronic neglect and abuse. They were kept and even tied in their cots, had very little social interaction, had no access to toys and play and were developmentally delayed in all areas. The children were also easily frightened and had learned to self-soothe through rocking and other means. This is an extreme example but it is indicative of the fundamental role of play in children's overall development and well-being.

Interestingly, other research on play deprivation shows that this and socio-economic deprivation are not necessarily linked. In other words, play is not dependent on economic well-being and material things. Where children have very little in the way of resources and toys, they will still find a way to play "everywhere and with anything" (Brown, 2012).

In this book, play is accepted and promoted as the most suitable "language" to use in a suite of parent–child programmes focused on improving attachment relationships through the fostering of RF. Bruce's words, quoted at the beginning of the chapter, show a synergy between the nature of play and RF; in the same way that RF describes an ability to "think, feel and act", so does play in Bruce's terms. For me, the partnership of play and RF is even more fundamental.

Play is a developmental process that crosses cultures and even species, in similar ways to attachment. Indeed, play is actually part of the way in which attachment can be seen to manifest in parent–child interaction.

When a child is securely attached to her parent or carer, she has come to learn that her "adult" (primary attachment figure) is dependable and predictable and seems to understand her in a good-enough manner. The child can then use her adult as a "secure base" from which to explore the world. Curiosity kicks in and she is happy to venture away from her base little by little to explore, play and learn. She might be happy to try that slide in the park, she might move away to pick up a plastic bottle and squish it to make a great noise, she might approach another child to play a game. When the child is big enough, she is happy to leave her safe adult even further away and out of direct contact. However, if the child becomes stressed, she will seek out her adult again, the one who makes her feel secure and safe. In this part of the attachment cycle, the adult is operating as a "safe place" to offer comfort and safety. When the child feels better, she will venture off again to play and explore.

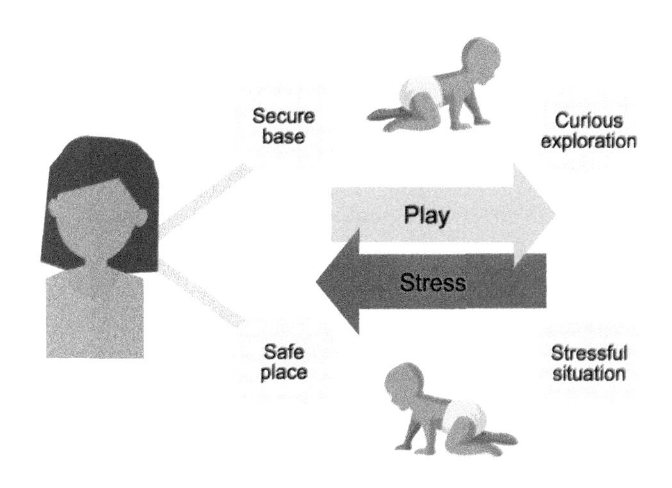

Figure 4.1: The Attachment and Play Cycle

Generally, children who feel safe and secure with an adult will learn over time to attribute these characteristics to other reliable adult relationships (secondary attachment figures) via their internal working model discussed in Chapter 2. These children will often settle at nursery, school and other familial and public settings in the care of other warm, consistent and predictable adults. They will often be curious children who will recover from stressful situations relatively easily and continue with the important playful business of being a child.

In this respect, attachment and play are inextricably linked on a number of levels and play is highly suited to provide the means by which to develop RF skills in families, both in attachment and child development terms.

For many children, play is just something that happens, but it has the potential for the emergence of properties that support survival and enhance well-being. Whilst the needs of older children and teenagers are different from those of young children, they are no less important. In the programmes in this book, "play" simply changes to reflect the developmental stage.

For example, in "baby bonding" the type of playful activity adopted reflects our understanding that sensitive and predictable parent–baby interactions – like body games (for example, "Round and round the garden"), face-to-face conversations and simple routines – are well-suited to newborns and very young babies (Murray, 2000). Babies have been shown to move quickly between six states in the early weeks and months after birth: deep sleep, light sleep, drowsy, quiet alert, unsettled and crying. In fact, babies are only ready to play when they are alert and quiet. Play in "baby bonding" is limited to times when babies are in the quiet alert state. In this programme, we support new parents to watch their little ones closely and respond to their needs in the moment. From around three months or so, and as babies' vision develops further, other baby toys and games are offered, for example home-made baby shakers and peek-a-boo games. The baby play in the quiet alert state is sensitive and parents are encouraged to see it as a "dance" between them and their baby as equal partners with close attention to the baby's individual preferences and signals.

In "toddler bonding", older babies are up and about and enjoying varying forms of free and structured play, from solitary to exploratory, parallel to stories, creative to imaginary and dressing up. As such, sessions include songs, rhymes, creative activities, loving touch, exploration and movement with parents and carers focusing closely on their toddlers' needs from moment to moment. During "toddler bonding" parents can be helped to understand the specific needs of toddlerhood and enjoy positive interactions including opportunities to help their toddlers make helpful choices.

"toddler bonding" is both active and calm and play is once again the sensitive dance between child and parent, with close attention to each toddler's preferences and signals.

In "heart-to-heart", the play has shifted considerably to reflect the needs of school-aged children and teenagers. Creative, fun, collaborative activities and games are offered which are developmentally appropriate and deeply respectful of all players. Everyone in the group can contribute to a group agreement that details a few agreed rules to help everyone relax and be clear on the boundaries. Play activity is structured but within each activity offered there is space for children to lead, make choices and determine outcomes for themselves.

Of course, children are all different and may need a flexible approach in the type of play offered. This approach is easily adapted to reflect the needs of individual families and children across the range of developmental needs and cultural contexts.

This book is squarely based on everyday play, which requires few resources – least of all special toys and gadgets. Programme resources are minimal, home-made, readily available and inexpensive. Again, they are easily adapted to culture and context.

The programmes are also built on play research which shows that, whilst children need to play alone and with peers, their parents and carers are a desirable and even favourite playmate (Baskett and Johnson, 1982). In addition, playing with children has a positive effect on parents and carers, increasing parental oxytocin levels (the "feel good" hormone) (Feldman, Gordon and Zagoory-Sharon, 2010).

Moving on now to look at how to implement the "baby bonding", "toddler bonding" and "heart-to-heart" programmes, the next chapter gives practical guidance and advice on how to set up these playful attachment programmes in a variety of ways including group and one-to-one work in clinical, community and home settings.

Chapter 4 headline messages

Play is a highly suitable and cross-cultural medium to use in a suite of parent–child programmes aimed at strengthening parental RF

Play can reduce children's stress levels and increase parental oxytocin levels

Play has been shown to be transformative in situations of extreme play deprivation and child neglect

Children will play instantaneously, for the sake of it, with anything and anywhere

Play is part of the way in which the attachment cycle is expressed and manifested between parent and carer and child

Parents and carers are important and significant playmates for children

Everyday and creative play requires few resources and many which can be easily found around the home and immediate environment

5

Reflective Functioning and Play programmes in the community: practical guidance for practitioners

> "And now here is my secret, a very simple secret: It is only with the heart that one can see rightly; what is essential is invisible to the eye."
>
> Antoine de Saint-Exupéry, *The Little Prince*

Introducing the suite of programmes

"baby bonding": for parents and carers and babies-in-waiting to babies-on-the-move (from 28+ weeks of pregnancy)

"baby bonding" is a group, one-to-one or home visiting RF programme for parents during late pregnancy (from 28 weeks onwards) and in the early months after the baby arrives. It can also be easily adapted for babies-on-the-move.

Pregnancy is the critical time to offer parents new information and emotional support. It is when parents generally start thinking about their growing baby inside and all the changes that her birth will bring. It is a window of opportunity in which parents who may not usually engage are open to new ideas and learning.

"toddler bonding": for parents and carers and toddlers

"toddler bonding" is a group, one-to-one or home visiting RF programme for parents and carers and their toddlers. It can also be easily adapted for early years and to support and prepare young children for the transition to school.

Toddlerhood can be a challenging time for families. This programme offers an opportunity to strengthen and support attachment security between parents and carers and toddlers through the nurturance of RF and its supports. Even where relationships have not begun well in infancy, toddlers are well able to adapt and remodel their attachment patterns in response to the consistent and predictable experiences of their parent or carer fostered by this programme.

"heart-to-heart": for parents/carers and school-aged children and teenagers

"heart-to-heart" is an RF programme for parents and carers and their children and teenagers. It can be delivered in group settings or one-to-one, including home visiting.

Covering a wide developmental period, "heart-to-heart" resources cover two approximate age ranges, six to nine years and ten to fourteen plus years. The primary aim of the programme is to strengthen attachment security in the parent–child relationship and to reduce the risk factors that threaten parental RF capacity.

Who can use these programmes and who are they for?

These programmes can be used by trained practitioners and professionals with the relevant skills, knowledge and experience of working with families and children. They are designed to build on existing practice that is already grounded in a comprehensive understanding of child development, attachment, play and family support. The programmes can be incorporated into existing work or be delivered alone. They are likely to appeal to social workers, health professionals, psychologists, family support teams, community development teams, portage workers, psychotherapists, play and creative arts therapists, teachers, play workers, early years specialists, international development workers, and a range of other suitably skilled professionals.

The programmes are designed and suitable for a wide range of families, whether as a universal or targeted approach. They are best seen as a preventative and early intervention approach and can be used as stand-alone or in conjunction with other services. Practitioners can use their professional judgement to assess the suitability of these programmes for individual families. However, they are unlikely to have the desired impact where attachment relationships are at deep crisis or breakdown point or where diagnosed psychological and/or mental health difficulties require urgent and specialist intervention. This said, these programmes can form part of a pathway through which families can move according to need. For example, a child and foster carer may need specialist support to settle a strained placement at risk of breakdown that can then be followed with relationship support using the "heart-to-heart" programme. Another example would be a group of mothers diagnosed with post-natal depression who were receiving a specialist healthcare service alongside or embedded within the "baby bonding" programme.

Session structure and rationale

The session *structure* is exactly the same for "baby bonding", "toddler bonding" and "heart-to-heart". This is because the structure relates directly to the active RF and attachment-generative mechanisms identified in the research. Each part of the session has a specific and explicit purpose rooted in the evidence base.

Thus, these programmes are *mechanised* and not manualised.

Whilst the structure below is outlined for a group context, each element is easily adapted for one-to-one and home visiting work.

However, the *content* of the sessions is necessarily very different across the three phases as appropriate for each developmental stage.

The session structure is as follows and is shown with the active research mechanism(s) alongside in brackets. Each mechanism relates directly to the evidence base discussed in Chapter 3:

- **Welcome** (Headspace and Containment). Sitting in a circle together each week (or side by side in a one-to-one setting), the welcome is designed to help parents, carers and children relax and signal the start of this time together. It could be a welcome song, a spoken welcome or hello game – everyone is greeted by name (we also say hello to babies *in utero* to affirm them as separate members of our group)
- **Group agreement** (Headspace and Containment). We agree a few simple positive rules together, for example mobiles off, respect each other, listen carefully to each other, choose how you want to join in, use kind words even if we don't agree, confidentiality unless a disclosure of risk to parent and/or child is made. On the first week we create this list of rules together. We never have a pre-made one because its creation is actually the process that maintains the boundaries throughout

the life of the group. We write it up and the group can help and even sign it if we know we are working with families who might find keeping to appropriate boundaries difficult. Stick it up on the wall each week and gently refer to and add to it if needed

- **Circle time** (Headspace and Containment). We then move on to a few "safe" and familiar activities which help the group relax and begin to feel safe together – playful rhymes, songs, games and low-key activities as appropriate
- **Breathing and regulation** (Regulation and Relaxation). Each week we acknowledge how hard it is being a parent and carer (and child/teenager!). We enjoy fun exercises designed to help us spend time breathing and regulating. We also draw attention to triggers that wind us up and share strategies to help calm and manage difficult and overwhelming feelings
- **Watching and wondering** (RF using Head, Heart and Hands and Behaviour, Meaning, Feeling). This is the section where RF is introduced little by little – often through very simple observation activities and games. For example, we might share how recent research has shown that actively thinking about our children can help strengthen our relationship. Then, we might ask parents to close their eyes and only think of "bananas" for one minute. When we all realise how hard it is to keep bananas in mind, it helps us focus and practise holding our children in mind with humour and greater application

We also move through the sequential stages of RF development outlined in the previous chapter

- **Loving touch** (RF using HHH and BMF). Each week there is a low-key activity which encourages positive and loving touch between parents, carers and their children and teens. This is through fun baby and toddler strokes and circle story massage. Alternatively, we use simple games, for example the child drawing a shape with her finger on her parent's back and then swapping. Touch can also be facilitated through objects if direct touch is not appropriate
- **A "gift" or "Bag of Ideas"** (Developmental knowledge). In each session we share ideas and information with parents and carers. There is an idea or small gift (for example a handout, poem, message, resource or DVD clip) to help nurture parents,

carers and children and send home important messages regarding children's development and emotional needs

- **Creative Relaxation** (Regulation and Relaxation). Each week parents, carers and children enjoy a creative relaxation exercise with calming music playing quietly in the background. I stick to the same story but you could vary it to suit. Many parents, carers and children find this activity unusual at the start but it often becomes a favourite part of the session. I have had teens say to me "Can we just do that sleeping thing?"
- **Try this at home** (RF using HHH and BMF). This is where we try very hard to encourage parents and carers to use RF at home with their children for just a few minutes each day. We suggest something to try each week. It is vital that the following week we ask them how they got on – good discussion usually follows
- **Brief recap on the day and see you next time** (Headspace and Containment). Recapping what we have done together in a session provides a gentle container. There is also a closing ritual, whether it is a song or a goodbye message, and we thank everyone for coming and taking the time out of their busy lives.

I usually run a session for an hour, with 50 minutes of activity and ten minutes to leave gently. After all, we have just spent time doing a creative relaxation! Those ten minutes also allow parents and carers to ask questions or talk to me a little more privately. We always start on time, but it is fine for parents to be late and just come in. Starting on time is another gentle container that helps families to regulate. They know they can come later, but generally parents and carers tend to become more regulated by gently holding to start and end times (along with the terms of our group agreement). Without this the session start time will slip.

The structure is set but the content is flexible and adaptable. The appendices provide practitioners with sample six-week programmes for babies, toddlers, children aged from around five to nine years, and older children and teens from ten to fourteen years. This represents a total of 24 sessions. However, some practitioners will need content for a one-off visit or session, whilst others may run a rolling programme in the community over many weeks. As long as practitioners have a very good understanding of the theory, evidence and purpose of each mechanism within the session, it is possible to use the programme in different ways.

The practitioner follows the session routine and populates it with appropriate playful activity. The activities can be changed or repeated as appropriate from session to session. In the early research, parents said that they liked the gentle routine of the session with changing activities within the overall framework. They liked that it was predictable and safe and that they got a sense week after week of how the session would feel. Interestingly, this was mirrored by the mood of the parents, carers and children, who became visibly more relaxed and contained as the weeks progressed (Maskell-Graham, 2009).

Setting up your group, one-to-one and home visiting work

All three programmes in this book can be used on a one-to-one basis with families and in small groups. They can be used for home visiting or take place in a number of settings, for example health and children's centres, community groups, nurseries, schools, and youth or clinical settings.

Programmes can provide content for a one-off session or visit, or run for a few weeks or over a school term. Most groups run for around eight weeks with five or six parent/carer and child pairs. The pilot "baby bonding" groups showed that eight sessions produced desirable results (ibid.). Ideally, groups have two practitioners but this is not always possible. The presence of two means that one can lead the activities whilst the other supports interactions and the RF process as it develops from moment to moment between parents, carers and children. If a lone practitioner is facilitating, she will have to fulfil both roles.

A containing environment

A containing environment is essential to the success of the programme and helps parents/carers and children to feel comfortable, safe and secure. This applies to both physical and emotional comfort.

Please consider the following as you plan your venue and space:

- A central location, preferably within walking distance for parents or with good transport links (the harder it is for parents and carers to get to the sessions, the harder it is for them to come at all)

- A venue with positive or neutral associations for parents – consider social, health and cultural factors
- Warm and comfortable room with curtains (for privacy and light management)
- Carpeting is ideal
- Relatively cosy space (large halls can feel uncontained)
- Breakout space (for changing/feeding – access to water)
- A space which is not easily interrupted and does not feel overlooked
- Easy access to toilets
- Access to drinking water and cups (NB: No hot drinks around children)

Working with your own soft "baby"

In "baby bonding" and "toddler bonding" the practitioner has her own "baby" to work with in each session. This is usually a baby massage doll, a soft doll or even a teddy bear. The baby is dressed in a simple nappy and Babygro® or similar, and is named.

In "heart-to-heart", children and teens are too big for this to be appropriate. Instead, we sometimes work in a practitioner pair and our working relationship embodies and models RF. However, it is also possible to deliver "heart-to-heart" alone. In this instance it is vital that, if you need to demonstrate a game or activity, you only do so with a willing parent or carer, never with one of the children or teens. This is to avoid you accidentally symbolising the "expert" parent and undermining the actual parent or carer.

The practitioner introduces her soft baby in the first session, explaining that this helps demonstrate and explain the activities in the group. Parents are very accepting of this idea. Some practitioners feel awkward working with a doll to begin with and so I recommend that you spend some time choosing, dressing and naming your baby. I also recommend that you have your own doll and do not share a central resource doll with other practitioners. If you have limited experience of holding small babies, I recommend using a realistic weighted doll, which helps you to support the baby convincingly and safely.

Your baby is absolutely essential to "baby bonding" and "toddler bonding" and plays a number of vital roles in the session:

- Most importantly, the practitioner uses the baby to model active RF and a secure attachment relationship; the baby is handled with warmth, care and sensitivity. This modelling is far more effective than advising a parent to behave in a particular way. It is also a highly supportive and non-judgemental way to model positive parent behaviours
- The practitioner gives her baby her own "voice" through RF, which is a vital tool in supporting parents to give their babies a voice
- The baby can be used to support parents when they find their baby's behaviour difficult. For example, a baby might start crying and the parent becomes stressed. We can contain and support the parent by mirroring the situation with our own baby. We can stand with the parent and rock our baby whilst the parent tries to comfort her baby. At the same time, we can still help the rest of the group to complete the original activity.
- We can model RF with our baby; we can do and say things that model to the parents that our baby's own thoughts and feelings are important and appreciated. For example, we can ask our baby's permission before we practise our baby strokes and follow her lead and preferences.
- We also use our baby to model the marked mirroring discussed in Chapter 3. For example, we pretend that our baby is frustrated and we use our face and voice towards her to accept this feeling. Our facial expression and voice "marks" the feeling in a slightly exaggerated way. If you watch parents with their children, you can often see them doing this quite naturally. The marking of feelings – positive and negative – allows babies to form a representation of the feeling without mistaking it for the parent's and becoming overwhelmed or frightened.

It is really important to keep your sensitive modelling going all through the session. For example, at the end of the session when you might be packing away and a few parents are still around, continue to handle your baby with care. It is best not to stuff your baby head first into a plastic bag in full view of the parents and carers!

In addition, bring a couple of spare dolls to each session for the parents to use. Pregnant parents may choose to enjoy activities using their own growing baby inside. However, they may also enjoy practising on a spare baby, for example practising some of the baby stroke activities. Spare babies also allow parents to truly follow their own baby's lead, which is essential to a group based on RF. If babies are asleep or not in the mood for an activity, a spare baby can be offered to a parent for practice. Parents feel validated that they recognise their own baby's cues, states and desires, and can still enjoy the activity with a spare baby doll. We need to avoid accidentally encouraging intrusive activity from parent or carer towards their baby. For example, "Round and round the garden like a teddy bear" is a favourite traditional rhyme in the UK and involves parents and carers drawing circles on the babies' palms or tummies. The final part of the rhyme involves tickling the baby. This tickling could be *highly* intrusive behaviour and parents need to feel well able not to conform to the activity if they feel that their baby does not wish to be tickled. We need to actively and explicitly encourage this in parents and carers. In this example, it is perhaps more likely that the baby will not want to be tickled at all.

Kit list

The kit should be kept as simple and portable as possible, containing only everyday items. We avoid specialist and expensive equipment because this models to families that they need special things in order to practise RF.

The kit usually consists of:

General kit:

- A soft floor covering (rug, blanket or similar), large enough for the whole group to sit on comfortably; a large duvet cover works nicely
- Optional cushions or pillows (squashed into a laundry bag or similar for ease of transport)
- Tablet or mobile phone preloaded with video clips, music and apps (consider social and cultural needs including resources in other languages); a Bluetooth mini-speaker or docking station may be used to provide increased volume for group work. I have found that virtually all parents around the globe now have a mobile phone and seem to use them a great deal. Instead of fighting technology, I try to use it to encourage positive interaction between parent and child. There are a number of excellent apps which can be used in the session and at home

to encourage RF. Music and songs can also be shared with parents through mobile phones

- Rhyme/song words. We will often make these into a group "songbook" and actively encourage parents and carers to teach us their favourite and traditional rhymes and songs. This works especially well when more than one language is spoken in the group. Parents will help write song words in the relevant language and phonetically to get the pronunciation right
- Developmental information – the "gift" of the week
- Posters for doors (to welcome attendees and to avoid interruptions during the session)
- Register/sign-in sheet/mobile phone numbers. I find that mobile numbers can change frequently so I keep track of these carefully. I also send a text message to families the day before along the lines of "Looking forward to seeing you tomorrow!" This acts as a container to help support regular attendance
- If appropriate, a welcome pack for new families: information letter, consent form and parent/carer details/contact sheet

Extras for "baby bonding" and "toddler bonding"

- Practitioner's own soft "baby"
- Two or three spare "babies" for parents and carers to use
- Changing mat
- A small basket of safe everyday "toys" for toddlers to explore if needed (for example comb, sponge, wooden spoon, tea towel, saucepan lid, scarf, pine cone)
- Bag of fabric pieces (tea towels, old ties, scarves, pillow cases, etc.)
- Bag of streamers (ribbons, tinsel, old ties, etc.)
- Old duvet cover, bed sheet or blanket (for "parachute" games)

Extras for "heart-to-heart":

- Bag of recycled materials for creative activities
- Safety scissors and tape
- Any activity- or game-specific materials

The kit is usually light, but practitioners are advised to store and carry their kit safely and carefully. Some practitioners have used light trolley bags that can be rolled along easily. A lockable cupboard in the venue is ideal for ongoing work.

Parents and carers of babies and toddlers should be asked to bring what they usually like to have with them when they are out and about with their children.

Open groups for all parents: a rolling health promotion programme model

An open, rolling health promotion programme is often a successful model for groups aimed at all local parents who would like to come along. Sessions are usually on a weekday at a helpful time for parents and carers, or sometimes a Saturday morning to encourage attendance by parents who work. Families can join and leave the group as convenient – it just keeps rolling along. There is generally a core group of parents who attend consistently. Community posters, leaflets and events listings can be used to advertise the group. These groups are sometimes funded (by the host organisation, for example a children's centre, charity, school or clinic), or parents make a small contribution (either weekly or for a fixed period).

Other types of open groups can also be run, for example a one-off weekend session for dads and babies, grandparents and toddlers, dads and sons, or mums and daughters. It may also be important to meet specific cultural needs, for example a women-and-babies-only group, or groups with the help of an interpreter. These can be designed to reflect local needs.

Groups for parents and carers who need extra support: a targeted programme model

Parents and carers who need additional support will usually benefit most from a closed group over a specific period of time, with eight weeks generally offering positive results. These parents and carers may share a specific need, for example, post-natal depression, or they may have children with particular needs. These groups will also benefit from an individual visit before the programme begins so that parents and carers can meet the practitioner, ask any questions and discuss anything they need to. This early relationship-building is likely to support attendance.

One-to-one work: a clinic or home visiting programme model

Where parents find it difficult to attend groups for a range of reasons or where need is high or complex, a home visiting programme is essential. Many of the parents and carers who might benefit most from these programmes are the very ones who will not access a group format. Practitioners need to work closely with health and social-work professionals to work out referral routes.

Practitioner skills

The success of these programmes rests on the delivery skills and personal attributes of the practitioners who facilitate them. No book can completely capture the level of interpersonal awareness, self-reflection and skill needed to underpin this work. These are the sort of skills best nurtured and practised in face-to-face experiential training and sustained through reflective practice and mentoring/supervision. Practitioners need to be a reflective, warm and predictable presence in the group. Essentially, the practitioner is going to be the benign and reflective mind needed to address and interrupt the problem of transmission gap discussed in Chapter 2. I always remind myself that people do what I do and not what I say, and that the most powerful way in which this programme is communicated is through authentic modelling on the part of the practitioner. I have to *be* the work rather than *do* the work.

The practitioner must work very hard at practising RF with group members. Once sessional content is underway, practitioners need to be watching, listening, noticing and reflecting on what is happening from moment to moment. This needs to be done highly sensitively so as not to draw attention to the parent or carer that could be unwanted or even unbearable. Non-verbal RF can sometimes be most powerful in holding a parent in mind.

Similarly, be careful about reflecting on a beautiful moment as it unfolds in front of you – this could completely ruin it. Instead, wait until the dyad bring their attention back to you or the group, then catch the parent's eye and smile; or maybe look warmly at their baby and reflect how special that connection was for them.

Practitioners can work hard at holding a group member in mind and imagining how things are feeling for them. They can gently catch the eye of the parent, carer or child and give a small smile or nod that lets them know that they are understood in that moment. If a parent or carer comes in looking and feeling tired and weary, the practitioner can invite her to sit down with a quiet reflection of how tough it is when we are worn out. If, as a practitioner, you notice some tension between a parent or carer and teenager, you can discreetly let them know that you understand that they are not comfortable with each other at that moment.

The practitioner does not rescue or try to fix any difficult feelings or thoughts in the group. The practitioner validates these feelings and thoughts, either verbally or non-verbally through a gentle nod of understanding or short statement that suggests that you understand that something is not quite right. Practitioners need to avoid two classic errors: making overlong spoken reflections and repeating verbatim what parents and children say.

The practitioner is one of the main containers of the group, and by being calm, warm, predictable and reflective the group's members feel safe within it. The practitioner also has the support of the group agreement to help keep the group contained. In order for practitioners to maintain these levels of skill and reflection in practice it is essential that they adopt the principles of reflective practice and have regular mentoring support from another experienced practitioner or clinician.

Reflective practice and practitioner mentoring

All practitioners adopting the programmes in this book are strongly advised to answer the following reflective questions soon after every session. The responses will provide rich material to guide future session planning and alert practitioners to where things are going well and not so well.

1. What went really well in today's session?
2. What seemed really hard in the session?
3. What feelings/reactions did I notice among parent, carer and child pairs?
4. How well did I contain the group – are any changes needed?
5. How well did I support RF in the group – any changes?
6. Any thoughts or ideas to take forward?
7. Any concerns about any parent, carer or child? (NB: Please follow your child protection policy and any other relevant policies and protocols)
8. Any points or worries to discuss with my mentor?

It is also a vital component of best practice for practitioners to have access to ongoing mentoring support from a more experienced fellow professional. This practitioner will be able to help you reflect and unpick the complex processes that are playing out in the sessions. This is also an important element of professional self-care and maintaining capacity to maintain the emotional life of the group or a particular pair. Finally, mentoring acts as a vital safety measure where practitioners are working with vulnerable groups or where there are child protection concerns.

Ethical practice

Practitioners need to adhere to and practise within a robust ethical and child protection framework. This extends to practical measures including insurance, contracting, licensing and practice policies.

The ethical principles that guide these programmes are respect, competence, responsibility and integrity. Each of these is expressed through a value statement which guides practitioner thinking, decision-making and behaviour.

Four ethical principles

Respect

Practitioners believe in the dignity and worth of all people regardless of difference, and are careful to uphold the individual rights of all those they work with. This includes parents, carers, children, other professionals, third parties and practitioners themselves. Self-respect and self-care are critical to the effective implementation of these programmes.

Competence

Practitioners work within the limits of their knowledge, skill, training, education and experience. When needed they refer to other professionals for guidance or refer parents/carers to specialist services. Reflective practice and professional mentoring are seen as essential to ensure competent working.

Responsibility

Practitioners value their responsibilities to the families they work with, the general public and the reputation of these programmes, including the avoidance of harm and the prevention of misuse or abuse of their position.

Integrity

Practitioners uphold honesty, accuracy, clarity and fairness in their interactions with families and all others during the course of their work.

Figure 5.1: Ethical value statements

Practitioners need to have comprehensive policies and procedures in place together with the relevant contracts, licences and insurance. Even where practitioners are working for an agency or other organisation, it is essential to check that the following are in place before any delivery with families begins:

1. Relevant insurance including public liability and professional indemnity
2. Risk assessment and risk-reduction measures (including venue)
3. Where appropriate, a contract with an umbrella or commissioning organisation or agency (for example, some practitioners may operate independently)
4. Suite of relevant policies including lone working and comprehensive child protection protocol arrangements (practitioners may work under an umbrella service whose policies they will need to adopt and can be detailed within contracting arrangements)

Practitioners will also need to be aware of and comply with any country-specific legal and practice guidance.

This chapter has detailed guidance for practitioners wishing to set up programme groups or one-to-one work in clinics and the community. The next chapter details the creative resources available to help practitioners deliver the programmes. There is also great scope to design your own lovely creative ideas.

Chapter 5 headline messages

The programmes in this book are designed to be used by trained practitioners and professionals and build on existing skills and knowledge in child development, attachment, play and family support

The programmes are best seen as a health-promotion or early intervention approach, or they can form part of a pathway of support for more complex families

These programmes are mechanised and not manualised. Their structure relates directly to the active RF and attachment-generative mechanisms identified in empirical research

Programmes can be used one-to-one with families and in groups in a number of health, community and agency settings

In terms of intensity and frequency of programme input, a routine of around eight weekly sessions has been shown to yield positive results

Practitioners work with their own soft "baby", who fulfils a number of essential roles within the session

Additional soft "babies" should be available for parents and carers to use during sessions to avoid difficulty in taking part in session activities if their child does not wish to participate

All items of programme kit are "everyday" and found in many homes

A home visiting or outreach model is likely to be essential for the families who may need these programmes the most

The success of the programmes rests on the delivery skills and personal attributes of the practitioner and particularly her ability to practise RF skills with the parents, carers and children

Reflective practice and practitioner mentoring are essential elements of these programmes

A robust ethical and child protection framework is essential including comprehensive policies, insurance and contracting arrangements

Programme resources

"But the eyes are blind. One must look with the heart."

Antoine de Saint-Exupéry, *The Little Prince*

Sample six-week programmes

"baby bonding", "toddler bonding" and "heart-to-heart" are flexible programmes that can be used to meet a range of developmental needs and family contexts. It is a mechanised approach, not a manualised one. The session structure is grounded in theory and driven by the active mechanisms identified in the current research evidence. This results in a session guided by a set of mechanisms that we know will support the development of RF in parents and carers and in turn strengthen the parent-child attachment relationship.

In order to support practitioners as they begin using this new approach, I have provided six example sessions for each developmental stage to illustrate the sessional and programme content. These can be found in the appendices at the back of the book.

It is vital that practitioners keep in mind that it is the session *mechanisms* that do the work. Effective sessions are those which activate and encourage these mechanisms – my advice is to keep it simple and focus on these rather than become overly preoccupied with complicated activities and resources.

Menu of ideas

In addition to sample six-week programmes, there is an online "menu of ideas" for each developmental stage. Each menu provides a host of different activity ideas for delivering the session mechanisms. Practitioners can pick their preferred ideas from each section to make their own individually-tailored session. Practitioners will also be able to use their own ideas to create sessional content.

Practitioner community and online resources

There is a practitioner community platform and resource bank which contain many resources to accompany this book; sample sessions, ideas menus, parental handouts, templates, video clip links and ideas, activity and gift ideas, and more. This resource bank is hosted by the UK charity "big toes little toes" at www.bigtoeslittletoes.org.

big toes little toes supports a growing number of practitioners specialising in RF, attachment and play. Its remit is to provide high-quality resources, training and mentoring and continuing professional development for those providing these specialist services to families around the globe. The charity is registered with the Charity Commission for England and Wales.

Practitioners trained in the programmes in this book can register with the practitioner community and access the online resource bank. They can also take advantage of free and affordable programme licensing arrangements, which come with a quality assurance mark. The practitioner community brings together a growing international community of practitioners around the globe who practise the programmes. It is a vital tool to share good practice, post new ideas and resources and be part of a supportive network.

In addition, revenue generated by programme training and support activities are used to fund delivery in a growing number of social projects in Africa and Asia.

This short chapter has focused on the programme resources available to support practitioners with their delivery. The appendices at the end of the book contain a total of 24 sample sessions across three developmental stages which act as a starting point for practitioners. We go on to look next at what practitioners can expect to happen during the delivery process with families. This includes how to deal with some of the challenges that may arise.

Chapter 6 headline messages

A total of 24 sample sessions are provided for practitioners in the appendices

Practitioners are advised to keep sessional content simple and focused on the known generative mechanisms

In addition to sample sessions, practitioners can access online resources to support their delivery

Online resources include "menus of ideas" that list multiple ways of delivering session mechanisms from which practitioners can design their own tailored sessions

An online resource bank hosts growing resources including parental handouts, links to video clips and ideas, developmental information, "gift" ideas and more

An online practitioner community provides a platform for practitioners to share good practice, post ideas and participate in a supportive global network

Online resources are currently hosted at www.bigtoeslittletoes.org

What should I expect?

> "Well, I must endure the presence of two or three caterpillars if I wish to become acquainted with the butterflies. It seems that they are very beautiful."
>
> Antoine de Saint-Exupéry, *The Little Prince*

Both practice and research show that parent–child pairs attending this suite of programmes tend to experience a four-stage process. It is useful to outline this process and the phases within it to help practitioners recognise and understand how best to support the developing work.

One of the most influential and popular models of the group developmental process was put forward by Tuckman (1965). Whilst there are various differences concerning the number of stages and their names, his model of four stages – forming, storming, norming and performing – has been widely adopted by practitioners. A fifth stage was added later: adjourning (Tuckman and Jensen, 1977) although, in the context of RF groups, mourning would appear to be a more appropriate descriptor.

To help bring the various phases of the group or individual processes to life, let me introduce two parent–child pairs: Grace and her baby, Anna (aged six weeks at the start of the programme) and Mandeep and his adopted teenage son, Rajan. In order to protect confidentiality, both cases are fictitious and draw from a number of real-life client experiences and testimonials.

First sessions ("forming")

In most one-to-one and group programmes, parents and carers are nervous or anxious at the beginning. There are a range of reasons for this, including anxiety about what will happen in a session, whether they will be judged an inadequate parent, whether their child will "behave" or show them up, whether they will be accepted by the other parents in the group, and a host of other concerns. First-time parents are often anxious about parenthood in general and attend to ensure that they have done everything possible and "correctly" to be a good parent.

Others are referred to programmes by professionals, including social workers and health visitors. Here there is often a genuine fear that parents may be exposed within the programme leading to serious consequences. Parents may be subject to court orders or child protection procedures and monitoring. Parents or carers may be separated from their partners and anxious about being identified as failing in some respect. Even parents who pay to attend a community group are often nervous or unsure at the beginning of the programme.

Grace is 32 and a first-time mum. Anna was born six weeks ago and is an unsettled baby, often awake and crying. Grace has heard about "baby bonding" from her health visitor and asks by email for details. She puts their names down for a new group starting alongside the baby clinic. Grace has found a big difference between her ideas of what motherhood would be like and the draining reality. She loves her baby daughter very much but finds it very hard to admit to anyone how low she feels.

A post-adoption agency runs a "heart-to-heart" programme for fathers and sons. Mandeep and Rajan are approached to attend. Mandeep is a quiet, reserved man aged 46. He and his partner were not able to have their own biological children. Rajan is now 13 years old and was adopted when he was three. He is unpredictable and sometimes lashes out at his dad. Mandeep finds this behaviour very difficult. Their social worker is struggling to find a suitable approach to support their strained relationship. They agree to come along, but neither is keen.

Whether real or imagined, anxiety is a key feature of the early sessions. My experience shows that this is the case even when parents present themselves as confident, defensive or (sometimes) aggressive.

From the moment I meet them, I practise my RF skills and imagine how hard it is to come and meet a professional for the first time. I smile and welcome parents and carers and thank them for coming. I will let them know that I appreciate that most parents and carers who come along are wondering about lots of things: What will the programme be like? What will the practitioner be like? Will she like and accept me? Will I like the programme? Will it help me? Gently pre-empting parental worries and identifying them as normal and common seems to be helpful. I also focus on listening hard to what parents are telling me and letting them know that they are understood.

If you are running a group, it is very useful to meet individual parents first or at least speak on the phone. From this, they will generally decide if you seem friendly, welcoming and professional and whether or not they are going to attend.

As parents, carers and children arrive for a session, meet them at the door (which should have a friendly welcome poster and a "Do not disturb" sign). Smile and greet them, help them understand where to go and where to leave their belongings in a safe and contained space. Invite them to join you in a circle when they are ready. Keep the entrance routine the same each week, and gradually everyone will make the transition into the working space with ease. Playing gentle and happy music quietly in the background also acts as a container for initial anxieties.

Grace and Anna arrive a little late for each session. Grace looks shattered and tries to calm an agitated Anna down. I notice that her default technique to soothe Anna is to feed her. She tucks herself away in the corner, starts to breastfeed Anna, and both seem to become calmer. Anna generally sleeps through the rest of the session. Her mum has her in her car seat next to her and practises all the baby bonding activities on one of our "spare babies" – some affordable multi-cultural soft baby dolls from a very well-known Scandinavian store.

Mandeep and Rajan arrive at the sessions on time each week. They sit together and join in the activities but I notice that there is an awkward atmosphere between them. Over the first couple of weeks, they seem to relax a little and they make friends with another dad and son pair. They seem relieved to have found others with things in common.

Early sessions ("storming")

The early research into these programmes showed that the first two weeks were generally the period when members of the group were getting to know one another and trying out some of the activities on offer. The group agreement, which was in place from the very beginning, had done a good job of containing everyone and their behavioural choices. Weeks 3 and 4, however, showed a shift. Group theory (Tuckman, 1965) describes a period of "storming" in which group members become more relaxed and secure in the group and their individual character traits become more obvious. Differences of opinion may also emerge and the group agreement becomes key in gently managing positive interactions, even in the face of disagreement. Parents in the early research also describe something fascinating. They said that they began to feel less pressure to present themselves as a "perfect" parent and were relieved with the "good enough parent" message that came through the group. In my research, I came to call this phenomenon the death of the "as if" parent or carer (Maskell-Graham, 2009).

Grace is visibly tired and tense and Anna is refusing to feed in order to sleep. Grace stands up with Anna, trying to rock and comfort her, but Anna just cries louder. The practitioner smiles at Grace, mouths "It's OK" and stands up with her soft baby to support Grace. Grace looks like she might burst into tears but then another baby starts crying too. The other mum also stands and the group gently laughs about how hard it is when the babies cry. One of the mums with a quiet baby says "I dread that he might start crying and you all think I'm a rubbish mum". Others agree and I notice that, though Grace says nothing, her shoulders have relaxed and she looks relieved.

Mandeep and Rajan arrive at the session and it seems clear that all is not well. Maybe they had an argument on the way or something else has happened. Mandeep sits down with a sigh and Rajan moves his chair further away from his dad. As we say our hellos, Mandeep sounds fed up and Rajan doesn't want to say anything today. One of the other dads pipes up and says, "I am so glad it's not just us that have a tough time even getting here!" Mandeep smiles and says "So it's not just us, then?" Others shake their heads and the practitioner reflects that he is very glad that everyone has come; things are not perfect in any family. The group continues and Mandeep and Rajan begin to try the activities together.

The concept of the "as if" personality is famously put forward by Miller (1987) and is essentially an adaptive or maladaptive defence mechanism. It could be described as an idealised aspect of the real self projected forward as a defence against a more fragile, congruent and honest self. Parents and carers attending programmes may often feel that they "should" know how to relate to their children. They may also feel under scrutiny from those around them. During the research, parents described a "letting go" of the ideal parent, which was associated with feelings of relief. This moment of letting go appeared to happen consistently in weeks 3–4 of the programme when parents were experiencing difficulties with their children in the group. It is difficult to know whether the tensions between parents and children and parents and parents caused everyone to relax generally and feel accepted for who they really were, or if, by relaxing, parents actually helped their children to be calm and relaxed. Possibly both processes were interacting. However, the result was a noticeable calming of the group dynamics and parents were feeling under much less pressure to present themselves in a particular way.

Later sessions ("norming" and "performing")

In this phase, groups tend to be well established and calm (even the babies!) Parents and carers generally arrive on time, engage well with activities and take ownership of their development. I like to think of it as doing myself out of a job! There are times during groups where activities and interactions are happening beautifully and I honestly think that no one would notice if I slipped out for a bit. Of course, this is not the case because I am a key symbol and container of this calm, predictable and reflective space. However, parents and carers are visibly empowered through their new understanding of their children. Children sometimes become more demanding of their parent/carer in the group, which I see as a great positive. Teens will make relaxed comments about their parents/carers, which previously the latter would have been unable to bear in the group context.

Parents/carers seem to have grown "bigger" and "kinder", with much broader shoulders. They feel more consistent and secure in their relationship with their child.

One key feature of these programmes is their attempt to bridge the transmission gap discussed in Chapter 2. In other words, these programmes must nurture parents and carers via the presence of a benign and reflective mind – the practitioner. If this part of the transmission gap is not addressed it will be very hard for the parent/carer to become the benign and reflective mind that their child needs.

Almost without exception, the favourite parts of the session become the relaxation exercise and the gift. Interestingly, teenagers seem to love these parts the most. These aspects of the programme are so very nurturing and containing. Rather than telling parents and carers and children what to *do*, they invite them to *be*; to practise being and becoming benign and reflective.

Grace arrives for the fourth session and visibly seems to relax as she comes through the door. "I like it here," she says. "It's a nice calm space." Anna is a little wriggly. Grace smiles at her and asks, "Hmmm. Is something the matter, little one? Shall I hold you like this and see if that helps?" Grace seems to be embracing the idea that she is an expert in Anna's care and pops her gently over her shoulder and rubs her back. Anna is still wriggling, so Grace smiles and changes her position again. "Is that better?" she asks Anna, who is now looking up at her mum's face.

Mandeep and Rajan come to the next few sessions and seem to be enjoying themselves more. The practitioner notices that they are laughing more together during some of the games and there is more spontaneous positive touch and non-verbal interaction. Interestingly, Mandeep is learning to step back a little and really listen to his son's thoughts and ideas. Rajan enjoys this and is starting to ask his dad to do things to help him. They come every week without missing a session.

Endings and outcomes ("mourning")

Members of many groups are sad when things come to an end. They have generally bonded together well and developed some strong relationships. The group has its own identity and has become a positive and predictable event in family routines. Some parents and carers worry that the support offered by the group is ending and they might not be able to sustain the things they have learned and enjoyed. Other parents are ready to end and may want ideas for what to do next. Some groups have gone on to meet up informally for coffee, whilst some members have joined alternative groups, and others have gone into "stay and play" or early learning sessions. The very first "baby bonding" group in Nottingham, which was formed for first-time mums in 2008, continues to organise its own get-togethers to this day and many more babies have been born since.

Grace and Anna arrive for the final session looking tired but relaxed. Everyone has brought a little something to share: cakes, fruit, biscuits, juice. The practitioner asks for everyone's favourite songs, games and stories and the session is a celebration of the individual journeys within the group. Grace is animated and makes a couple of suggestions. All the parents have ideas about how they might stay in touch and the practitioner hands out some information about other local baby-friendly groups. Grace and a couple of others agree to meet up for lunch after the session. Anna is peaceful and alert throughout. She is sitting on her mum's lap and looking around. She particularly likes looking at the home-made baby shaker her mum has made for her. Grace seems really happy with her programme certificate and, though shy, still enjoys getting a clap from all the other parents.

Mandeep and Rajan bring to the final meeting some cookies they made together at home. They even iced them with the initials of everyone in the group. Everyone else is really impressed! The practitioner asks group members for some of their favourite moments and shares some photos that the group took on disposable cameras one week. The group enjoys putting some photos into an album and decorating the cover with their names and some stickers. The practitioner asks if they would like to meet up again in a few months to see how everyone is. The group suggest that they meet up at a local park for a picnic and some friendly games. Mandeep and Rajan also arrange to meet another dad and son the following week.

Common challenges

Of course, programmes do not always go smoothly and some common challenges do crop up now and again. Examples of these are listed below, along with some suggested strategies to try out.

1. *One parent dominates the group and regularly talks over other parents and carers.* The group agreement is in place and the practitioner refers to it and asks everyone to respect other group members. The practitioner can also position him/herself next to the parent (acting as a container), thank the parent for their first contribution and then invite others to contribute their thoughts and ideas.
2. *One parent is extremely anxious and asks lots of questions about how to get her toddler to sleep at night.* The practitioner reflects that many parents are worried about sleeping, with good reason. Perhaps this parent would like an appointment with the health visitor to work through suggestions that might help. Or could the practitioner organise for the health visitor to come along at the end of the session one week to address issues and concerns?
3. *Two parents come together and obviously know each other really well. They always want to work together rather than with other group members.* The practitioner can ensure that the group agreement established at the start of the programme explains that everyone should work with each other throughout the group rather than stick with who each knows. Another idea is to have a bag of stones or buttons for people to pick out, which sorts them into mixed

groups. Or use circle time activities to swap places and speak to everyone.

4. *There is a parent that the practitioner is very worried about and does not seem to be responding to the group content and process.* The practitioner might spend a few minutes alone with this parent at the beginning or end of the session or arrange a meeting outside the group to talk things through. Additional referrals may be needed to meet the full range of needs.

5. *A carer discloses some very sensitive information about something that happened to him/her as a child.* The practitioner reflects how important it was for this carer to share this information, reiterates to the group that this information must remain confidential, and offers to spend time with the carer after the group to talk it through fully. Professional advice and/or an additional referral may be needed.

6. *The practitioner is very concerned about the safety of one of the parents and his/her children but there has been no disclosure.* The practitioner follows the protocols for raising concerns, including getting advice from the designated safeguarding lead.

7. *There is a parent in the group who does not speak in discussions but seems perfectly happy to be in the group.* The practitioner ensures that there are lots of different ways to join in discussions; for example, Post-it® notes or a postbox for thoughts, ideas and suggestions, or time to speak to the practitioner at the end of the session.

8. *There are mixed languages in the group and a couple of parents have little English.* The practitioner has already planned for this and has appropriate songs, games, activities and resources planned and translated. The practitioner speaks English as a first language but has found out how to greet the group in the different languages spoken. The group really appreciates this, even if the practitioner doesn't get it quite right. The group helps everyone learn the traditions of the countries represented and together makes a special multi-lingual group songbook to keep.

9. *A parent is openly critical of their toddler in the group.* The practitioner reflects that we all struggle with our children at times and it can be very hard when this is in public. She continues that this is a group in which everyone accepts and respects everyone else, including the little ones, without passing judgement. The

> practitioner might then give the toddler their voice and reflect how hard it is when things are not going well with mummy. The group then moves into another activity and the practitioner offers support to the pair as needed.

This chapter has outlined the process that most groups go through over the life of a programme. This can also be seen in one-to-one work in which the "group" is the practitioner, the parent/carer and the child. This process is neither positive nor negative. In other words, just because a group is going through a stormy patch does not mean that the practitioner is not doing a good job. In fact, quite the opposite. The practitioner has created a safe and contained environment in which parents and carers (and children) begin to relax and become their true selves. Storming is inevitable, even in subtle ways, and is very positive. The trick is for practitioners to recognise that the group is growing and moving forward. If the practitioner contains any struggles, personality clashes and behaviour challenges in a predictable and contained way, the group will move through this phase and begin to grow and develop in exciting and less stressful ways.

We will now go on to examine how programme commissioners and practitioners can evaluate and measure the impact of these programmes. We look at how we can measure changes in parental RF capacity, and the challenges of doing this in practice rather than in research settings. We also look at how we can measure other important factors including the known supports and stressors affecting RF.

Chapter 7 headline messages

Parent–child pairs attending these programmes either one-to-one or in groups appear to experience a four-stage process: forming, storming, norming and performing

Pre-empting and normalising parental concerns and worries about attending seems to help reduce anxiety

Initial (and ongoing) contact with the parent or carer (initial meeting, phone, email, text) is helpful in supporting attendance

Weeks three and four are sometimes hard for parents and carers and associated with them embracing the idea of the "good-enough" parent

Endings are very important and need to be managed sensitively and well

Challenges are common and part of a positive process

Assessing programme impact

"You know ... my flower ... I am responsible for her. And she is so weak! She is so naïve! She has four thorns, of no use at all, to protect herself against all the world"

Antoine de Saint-Exupéry, *The Little Prince*

Most practitioners will be required to measure the impact of these programmes, especially where they are funded externally. However, there is a substantial difference between those measures intended for research purposes and those available for use in practice. For example, standardised and validated measures of RF used for research purposes generally require specialist training and certification and a substantial interview between parent and researcher.

The gold standard measure for assessing parental RF is the Parent Development Interview (PDI) (Aber et al., 1985; Slade et al., 2002, 2005), which can be used at varying data collection points during a research study. Parental Embodied Mentalising (PEM) (Shai, 2010) is also highly recommended for research purposes.

However, as these measures are not easily available to practitioners running programmes on the ground with families, suggested self-reporting questionnaires are listed below. These can be used before and after programmes to help assess programme efficacy. In discussion with commissioners and managers, decisions can be made about which measures are most suitable. I have used all of the suggested measures with parents and carers (and some with older children and teenagers) and found them useful to collect quantitative data for tracking progress and generating final reports.

However, it is also vital to collect the personal experiences and stories of families through the programmes. I have done this in various ways, including an end-of-programme evaluation form, individual and group discussions that are recorded and transcribed, and a short telephone interview. Families have also enjoyed creating paintings, poems and "word clouds" when invited to share their thoughts and feelings about their programme journeys. Qualitative data have been used to supplement and illustrate the quantitative data.

The suggested quantitative measures below are in the public domain, but do ensure that the necessary permissions and referencing requirements are in place as appropriate. These measures are suggested because they are well validated, generally available and quick and easy for parents and carers to complete and practitioners to score and interpret. It is essential to have data control and protection protocols in place in accordance with the Data Protection Act 1988 or other national frameworks.

"baby bonding" and "toddler bonding" measures

1. *Mothers Object Relations Scale (Oates and Gervai, 2003)*

This 14-item questionnaire is a screening tool for identifying potential areas of difficulty in the early mother–infant relationship. It assesses maternal perceptions of infant "warmth" and "invasiveness". It is easy to use and can be printed out as parent-friendly booklet. I find that parents and carers find it non-threatening, and straightforward to complete. This tool has been shown to possess stable and internally coherent scales. Specifically, internal consistency has been shown to be >0.70 (Simkiss et al., 2013). This scale is currently the only psychometric instrument available that assesses a mother's representations of her relationship with the infant/toddler. This is important in the context of RF, which is based on parental conceptualisation of the child.

2. *Maternal Antenatal Attachment Scales and Maternal Postnatal Attachment Scales (Condon, 1993)*

The Maternal Antenatal Attachment Scale is a self-reporting measure containing 19 items rated on five response options focusing on the frequency and/or intensity of these experiences over the preceding two weeks. It takes a little while for parents and carers to complete, and sometimes parents prefer me to read it out to them. Encouraging parents to be as honest as possible is very important, along with reassurance that there are no right or wrong answers. Practitioners also need to be careful not to lead parents and carers to answer in a particular way and to have a neutral response to their answers.

The scale is used during the third trimester of pregnancy and was developed to measure maternal bonding with the infant. Condon noted that, as the pregnancy progresses, the pregnant woman would normally be expected to develop an increasingly elaborate internalised representation of the baby (Condon, 1993). This would in turn facilitate the growth of the parental emotional bond with the unborn infant. The 19 items for the maternal scale focus on feelings, attitudes and behaviours of the pregnant woman towards the baby, with responses recorded on a five-point Likert Scale. Two subscale scores are derived from the items: quality of attachment and time spent in attachment mode, which can be classified as four discrete types (positive-preoccupied, positive-disinterested, negative-preoccupied and negative-disinterested). A total attachment score can also be calculated. Adequate internal consistency has been demonstrated, with a Cronbach's alpha of >.80 (ibid.). This scale has been suggested because of its predictive value of post-natal attachment when the baby is in early infancy (Condon and Corkingdale, 1998).

The Maternal Postnatal Attachment Scale is the accompanying self-reporting measure to assess the affective aspect of the mother-to-infant relationship in the infant's first year of life. The theoretical framework underpinning the development of the questionnaire is similar to that for the Maternal Antenatal Attachment Scale above.

A total attachment score can be calculated, along with four subscales: pleasure in proximity to the infant and enjoyment during interaction with her; acceptance of the infant and a lack of maternal resentment of the impact on the mother's lifestyle; tolerance of the infant and absence of angry or hostile feelings towards the infant; and feelings of competence and confidence as a parent. A total score is also generated. The authors report very good internal consistency reliabilities (alphas) of 0.78–0.79 (Condon and Corkingdale, 1998).

3. Hospital Anxiety and Depression Scale (HADS) (Zigmund and Snaith, 1983)

This is a 14-item scale for detecting clinically significant depression and anxiety in outpatient settings. It is widely used with clinical populations and is useful because it excludes items that might reflect physical illness. It is relatively easy for parents and carers to complete.

The screening tool's 14 items are rated on a four-point Likert Scale, ranging from 0 to 3. The instrument comprises two separate scales

– Anxiety (HADS-A) and Depression (HADS-D) – with seven items in each scale and a maximum score of 21 points. Cut-off scores allow for categorisation into normal, mild, moderate and severe states for the two factors. A review of studies using this scale showed satisfactory psychometric properties (Bjelland et al., 2002). Validity for "caseness" was established, and internal reliability as measured by Cronbach's alpha for the HADS-A ranged between 0.68 and 0.93, with a mean of 0.83.

HADS is suggested over other measures of anxiety and/or depression precisely because it differentiates clearly between the two domains. Other measures, such as Edinburgh Postnatal Depression Scale (Cox et al., 1987), do not allow for the differentiation between anxiety and depression, which is likely to be an important distinction in the ranking of variables in order of importance or impact on RF.

"heart-to-heart" measures

1. Strengths and Difficulties Questionnaire (SDQ) (Goodman, 1997)

The SDQ is a brief behavioural screening questionnaire used for 3–16-year-olds. It exists in several versions and languages to meet the needs of researchers, clinicians and teachers.

Parents and carers generally find it easy to complete and seem to like the questionnaire. It seems to validate parental concerns about their child's behaviour.

The SDQ asks about five attributes in each of five scales (i.e. 25 in total): emotional symptoms, conduct problems, hyperactivity/ inattention, peer relationship problems and pro-social behaviour. Scores are generated for total difficulties and pro-social behaviours. The same 25 items are included in questionnaires for completion by the parents and/or teachers of 4–16-year-olds (Goodman, 1997). There is a slightly modified version for the parents and/or nursery teachers of three- (and four-) year-olds.

A further version for self-completion by adolescents asks about the same 25 traits, though the wording is slightly different (Goodman, Meltzer and Bailey, 1998). This self-reporting version is suitable for young people aged around 11 to 16, depending on their level of understanding and literacy.

Extended versions of the SDQ are available, which also assess the impact and chronicity of recorded difficulties.

2. TOPSE (Tool to measure Parenting Self Efficacy) (Kendall and Bloomfield, 2005)

TOPSE was developed as a tool to measure parenting self-efficacy and is used in both the UK and many other countries to evaluate a range of parenting programmes and interventions. It was developed in the UK in response to demand from public health practitioners who identified the need for a reliable and valid instrument to assess the outcomes of programmes to support parents and carers. It can be printed out as a booklet and is accessible and easy for parents and carers to complete.

TOPSE consists of 48 self-efficacy statements across eight domains: emotion and affection; play and enjoyment; empathy and understanding; control; discipline and boundary setting; pressures of parenting; self-acceptance; and learning and knowledge. There are six self-efficacy statements for each domain and parents show how much they agree with each statement by responding to a Likert Scale from 0 to 10, where 0 equates to completely disagree and 10 equates to completely agree.

Parents complete the TOPSE booklet at the first session of a programme and again in the final session to determine any change in self-efficacy scores. The programme facilitator reassures each parent that there are no right or wrong answers and that parents are not being compared against each other. TOPSE may also be sent to parents four to six months following the programme to establish whether changes in self-efficacy have been maintained.

3. Parenting Daily Hassles Scale (Crnic and Booth, 1991)

This scale aims to assess the frequency and intensity/impact of 20 potential parenting daily "hassles" experienced by adults caring for children. It has been used in a wide variety of research studies concerned with children and families – particularly families with young children. It has been found that parents and carers generally like completing it because it touches on many aspects of being a parent that are important to them. However, some practitioners may not like it because it could seem to emphasise negative traits in the child.

"Tell me about your baby/child": a clinical tool

I have also designed a relatively quick and easy method for gathering pre- and post-programme data which gives an *indication* of parental RF capacity. It is especially suited to a short pre- and post-programme meeting with parents/carers that also includes sharing information about the programme and the completion of any other questionnaires.

"Tell me about your baby/child" is a very short exercise in which each parent or carer is asked to speak about her baby or child for one minute only. This includes asking expectant parents to talk about their growing baby-in-waiting. Parents and carers give their permission for this data to be collected, recorded (I suggest usually on a mobile phone or tablet) and stored securely under the relevant data protection legislation.

The practitioner uses the following prompt: "Please tell me about your baby (child) and what they seem to be like". The parent then speaks without further questions or comments from the practitioner. The practitioner listens carefully, showing neutral acceptance of all statements made. When the minute ends the practitioner thanks the parent.

The practitioner transcribes the recording and uses the following method to code the transcript:

1. She reads the transcript through once.
2. On the second reading, she highlights any "thinking" or "feeling" words, either the parent's thoughts and feelings or those of the baby or child. Each highlighted word is read again in context and the following scores are given:

    a. Baby's/child's thoughts and feelings (score 1 per example)

    b. Parent's/carer's thoughts and feelings (score 1 per example)

    c. Where parents recognise that their thoughts and feelings affect their baby/child (score 2 per example)

    d. Where parents recognise that their baby's/child's thoughts and feelings affect their thoughts and feelings (score 2 per example)

For example, the transcript reads: "I'm not sure but I think my baby gets bored sometimes". The practitioner highlights "think" and "bored".

"think" is the parent's thought word and scores 1.

"bored" is the baby's feeling word and scores 1.

There is no indication here that the parent recognises that her thoughts and feelings affect her baby – score 0.

There is no indication here that the parent recognises that her baby's thoughts and feelings affect her own – score 0.

Second example: "I think my child gets bored with me and this makes me feel guilty and useless". The practitioner highlights "think", "bored", "guilty" and "useless".

"think" is the parent's thought word and scores 1.

"bored" is the child's feeling word and scores 1.

There is no indication that the parent recognises that her thoughts and feeling affect her baby – score 0.

The parent shows recognition that her child's feeling of being "bored" makes her feel "guilty" and "useless" – score 2.

1. The score is totalled to give an indication of the parent's or carer's RF capacity
2. Enter the parental score into a spreadsheet
3. Re-do the measure at the end of the programme and compare the pre- and post-scores
4. Graphs can be generated to show score changes across time and between score domains.

An increase in score is indicative of an increase in RF, no change in score is indicative of no change, and a decrease in score is indicative of a reduction in RF.

For practice purposes, a total score of 0 to 2 can be considered low, a score of 3 to 5 adequate and 6 or more high.

Please note that the parent's or carer's thinking and feeling words are not assessed for their positive or negative implications. We just want a quick idea of whether this parent has a reflective capacity. In other words, parents and carers can say things that appear negative, for example "I don't think my baby likes me much. I am sure she cries at night just to annoy me". Whilst this statement might alert us to problems in the relationship, it would still score reasonably well on RF capacity. We are not looking for "good" or "bad" RF, but for an ability to do it at all. Similarly, parents and carers could give an over-positive response, perhaps worrying about what a "good" parent is supposed to say; for example, "My baby is very good, she sleeps all through the night and doesn't make much fuss at all". Once again, it is the reflective capacity we are looking for rather than a good or bad narrative. This last example has no RF language yet presents a positive situation. However, if parental statements are distorted, either positively or negatively, this gives us very useful additional information about the nature of the parent–child relationship.

Please note that "Tell me about your child" is a practice measure designed to assist practitioners to measure possible programme impact on RF capacity. A validation study is planned.

Programme evaluation and case studies

A number of university evaluation studies to explore the impact of this approach have been carried out. There is also a growing number of practitioner case studies which share specific examples of how the programmes have been used in a number of settings around the globe.

For example, the programmes were first piloted in Nottingham, UK, as a universal health promotion approach. Following their success and additional research into the attachment change mechanisms, they were then adapted for work in the Obunga slum in Kisumu, Kenya. This work has since expanded throughout the slum, into neighbouring rural villages and across the border into Uganda under the aegis of the UK charity Lullaby Africa.

"baby bonding" has been effectively implemented with women and their babies on the border between Thailand and Myanmar who are at high risk of being trafficked. This work is partly funded by "baby bonding" programmes running as a health promotion approach in private health clinics and educational settings.

In addition, local authority-funded "toddler bonding" programmes in community settings have been seen to strengthen relationships between foster carers and toddlers in rural Ireland. A rolling programme of "baby bonding" has been offered to vulnerable women and their very young children in women's refuges in Cape Town, South Africa. Universal community programmes have also been running to great effect in various locations as a health promotion approach.

As new evaluation and case studies are underway and also in the planning, this growing evidence base is hosted online as part of the resource bank signposted in Chapter 6.

This chapter has outlined a number of measures and methods available to commissioners and practitioners to evaluate programme impact across a range of ages and domains. Whilst the programmes themselves are relatively new, they are built on a significant body of research which identifies the generative mechanisms needed for positive attachment change. Specific programme evaluation is underway and ongoing. As we advance to the concluding chapter, the focus moves to the need for early intervention to offer children the best possible outcomes and the importance of fidelity to the programme mechanisms.

Chapter 8 headline messages

Robust evaluation is essential to measure programme efficacy and impact

RF measures designed for use in research are not always easy or appropriate for practice use

A number of validated self-reporting measures are suggested for pre- and post-programme use

Capturing parental experiences, thoughts and views is as important as measuring efficacy with quantitative measures

"Tell me about your child" is a new one-minute exercise that gives practitioners an indication of parental RF capacity

Practitioners need to focus on parental capacity for RF rather than be distracted by a positive or negative narrative

Positive or negative parental narratives give us additional information about the nature of the parent–child relationship

A number of university programme evaluation studies have been completed or are being planned

Evaluation study summaries and global case studies are regularly added to the online resources which accompany these programmes

Conclusion

This book has set out the theory, evidence base and structure of a new suite of programmes based on RF and play. Its main purpose is to strengthen attachment relationships between parents, carers and their children from late pregnancy to teens through three playful and accessible programmes.

Whilst the approach is relatively new, it is evidence-based and built on known attachment mechanisms derived from a detailed literature review and synthesis of over 140 recent peer-reviewed studies up to and including early 2016. Emerging programme results are positive across a number of cultures and settings.

In addition, both play and attachment are accepted developmental processes that are relevant and appropriate for family work across cultures. They are even shown to be relevant across mammalian species.

Offering a comprehensive book and accompanying online resources comes from a desire to make this approach widely available to a range of professionals with relevant experience and skill. Many practitioners working with families will be able to make use of this approach and interweave its principles into their existing work.

However, it is vital that the integrity of the approach is maintained, or it will not deliver the kind of relationship change that families and practitioners hope for. No matter how good the book or online resources and ideas might be, it is the quality of the practitioner's delivery and her relationship with the parent or carer that will make or break this work.

It is essential that practitioners using this approach are fully trained, highly skilled and experienced. Affordable training in these programmes is offered in the UK, online and in a growing network of venues around the globe. Regular continuing professional development is also recommended to keep practitioners up to date with developments within the field. Finally, practitioner self-care is essential to establish and maintain both the skills required to run these programmes and the joy of working with families.

The strength of this book is the way in which it takes theory and validated research, identifies the attachment mechanisms at work and turns these into practical everyday play activities. Practitioners need to be well versed and confident in the theory and research knowledge underpinning these.

I do hope that you enjoy using this approach with families and watch parents and carers begin to blossom into who they really want to be. I also hope that parents and carers begin to feel truly empowered as the experts in their children's growth and development.

Our children are not in control of their earliest relationships so it is essential to support families as early as possible and not wait for problems to become entrenched and really hard to unpick. We need to support parents and carers to be the best they can, so that our children fulfil their amazing potential.

Finally, I continue to hope for social change built on the respectful, loving and containing relationships that this book promotes. Our society would indeed be a much happier and kinder place.

Debi Maskell-Graham

> "There can be no keener revelation of a society's soul than the way in which it treats its children."
>
> Nelson Mandela, 1995

Appendix 1

A programme for parents, carers and their babies-in-waiting and babies (from 28+ weeks of pregnancy)

Six sample sessions

"baby bonding": Week 1
"Welcome to 'baby bonding'"

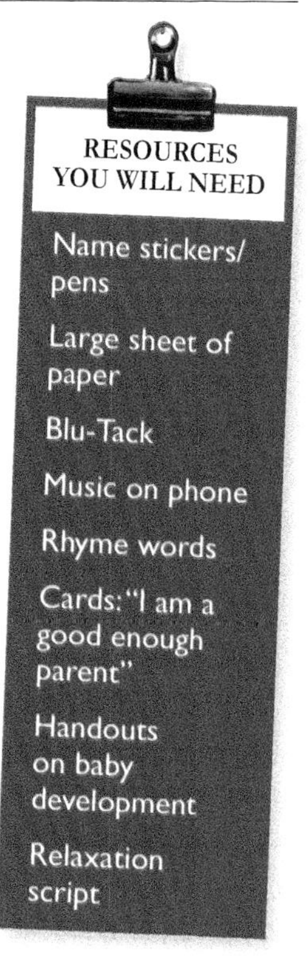

Welcome (Headspace and Containment)

Invite parents/carers and babies to come and sit with you in a circle – parents make name badges for themselves and baby if born (baby badge on parent under their name). Welcome everyone and thank them for coming. Explain that the programme is based on the latest research on attachment and that over the weeks we will be enjoying this together.

Introduce and sing a hello song (your own or from online resource bank).

Group agreement (Headspace and Containment)

Invite parents to help you write a short list of things that will help the group go well and to be a safe place for all; stick it up on a wall. Examples: mobiles on silent, listen to each other, respect for all, follow our baby's lead, what we say in the room stays in the room, etc.

Circle time (Headspace and Containment)

Gently introduce the "baby bonding" session structure – begin with a few simple rhymes, songs or activities each week. Start by repeating a familiar and appropriate rhyme with actions; ask parents to watch their baby (or think about their baby inside) to see what position they like or if they enjoy the actions – encourage them to change in response to their baby's wishes. Examples of songs: "Eensy Weensy Spider", "The Grand Old Duke of York".

HINT: Model the rhyme very sensitively with your own baby, asking the baby's permission and responding to her wishes and preferences.

Breathing and regulation (Regulation and Relaxation)

Explain that we understand that being a parent of a small baby is very hard and tiring; invite parents to take some deep breaths in and out and gently share how important it is that we take time to breathe when things are tough. Breathe in through your nose if you can and out through your mouth. Place your hands on your ribs and feel the breath pushing your ribcage and hands out and then in again. Practise together for a few minutes.

Watching and wondering (Head, Heart and Hands)

Ask parents to either hold their baby or lay her down – whatever they think their baby needs right now. Expectant parents should make themselves comfy. Ask them to just spend time thinking about and watching their baby – *really* watching them. Notice if you start thinking about other things! Come back to your baby and practise. Explain that research shows that parents who spend time really watching and thinking about their babies begin to understand their signals better and feel more of an expert in their own child – even tiny babies.

Over the weeks, we will practise techniques together and learn more about how to strengthen our baby's attachment relationship to us.

HINT: Quiet, calm music; model carefully with your own baby; notice what is happening in the group and reflect gently. For example, "Some babies are really enjoying this and others not so much – you are noticing and adapting really well".

Loving touch (Head, Heart and Hands)

Invite parents to place their baby in front of them and then to ask the baby for permission to try some loving baby touch. Expectant parents can touch their baby inside and/or practise on a "spare baby". Place both hands on your baby's chest and take some really deep breaths – imagine that you are sending your breath into your baby, peacefully and deeply. Practise the "velvet cloak" baby stroke – or another simple baby stroke (see online resources).

HINT: Model carefully – music still on in background.

A "gift" or "Bag of Ideas": sharing ideas and information with parents and carers (Developmental knowledge)

Each week, we share a gift or idea with parents – something to nurture parents and also share important information about babies. Give out a small card to each parent that reads "I am a good enough parent" – create your own or find a template in the online resources. Explain that attachment theory is really clear – babies need us to be good enough, and not perfect! Enjoy chatting this through if parents want to discuss.

Handout: a lovely information sheet on 0-to-two-month-olds – be sensitive to literacy/language, etc. (available as a PDF from the online resource bank).

Creative relaxation (Regulation and Relaxation)

Explain that each week we enjoy a creative relaxation together – see suggested script online.

HINT: Deliver script in a calm voice and at a gentle pace, with music on in the background.

Try this at home (Head, Heart and Hands)

Ask parents to practise watching their baby for a few minutes each day at home; next week we can catch up and see how we got on.

Brief recap of the session, and see you next time (Headspace and Containment)

Just recap what we have covered today and thank parents for coming and taking the time out of their busy days. End with a "goodbye and see you next week".

"baby bonding": Week 2 "Babywatching"

Welcome (Headspace and Containment)

Invite parents/carers and babies to come and sit with you in a circle – name badges for parent and baby.

Welcome everyone and thank them for coming.

Hello song.

Group agreement (Headspace and Containment)

Invite parents to remember our agreement – did it work OK? Anything to add? Stick it up on a wall.

Circle time (Headspace and Containment)

Start with repeating last week's familiar rhyme; ask parents to think about and watch their baby to see what position they like or if they enjoy the actions; encourage them to change in response to their baby's wishes. Example rhyme: "Eensy Weensy Spider", "The Grand Old Duke of York".

Add a couple of new rhymes or simple songs (e.g. "Twinkle, Twinkle, Little Star").

HINT: Model the rhyme very sensitively with your own baby, asking the baby's permission and responding to her wishes and preferences.

Breathing and regulation (Regulation and Relaxation)

We are going to practise our breathing again; invite parents to take some deep breaths in and out. Add music and encourage parents to feel their ribcage expanding and contracting with their breaths. Each breath becomes deeper.

This week we add a safeguarding message to encourage parents that becoming overwhelmed by difficult feelings as a parent is normal

– it is what we do about it that counts. If breathing doesn't help you calm down, a good enough parent will put their baby down somewhere safe and walk away to calm down for a few minutes.

Watching and wondering (Head, Heart and Hands)

Ask parents to either hold their baby or lay her down – whatever they think their baby needs right now. Ask them to just spend time watching their baby – *really* watching them. Notice if you start thinking about other things! Come back to your baby and practise. Give out "baby thought bubble" sheets to help parents think about their baby's thoughts (see online).

HINT: *Quiet, calm music; model carefully with your own baby – notice what is happening in the group and give babies a voice, e.g. "You are watching Mummy so carefully, Meena".*

Loving touch (Head, Heart and Hands)

Invite parents to place their baby in front of them and then to ask the baby for permission to try some loving baby touch; expectant parents choose own growing baby inside or spare baby.

Place both hands on your baby's chest and take some lovely deep breaths – imagine that you are sending your breath into your baby.

Practise the "velvet cloak" baby stroke – add two or three new strokes.

HINT: *Model carefully – music still on in the background.*

A "gift" or "Bag of Ideas": sharing ideas and information with parents and carers (Developmental knowledge)

Using a tablet or laptop, show Warwick Medical School's DVD clip on the six baby states (www.your-baby.org.uk).

There are lovely baby books that can be used as a low-tech alternative, for example *Global Babies* (The Global Fund for Children/ Charlesbridge, 2007) and *Baby Day* (Bookstart, Little Tiger Press, 2013), or use photos of baby and toddler faces.

Now go around the group and have some fun guessing what states our babies are in right now! Encourage parents to babywatch during the week and feel that they can recognise how their baby is feeling.

Encourage parents to initiate play only when babies are quiet and alert, and to notice if they turn away or become overwhelmed. Small babies will sometimes hiccup, regurgitate milk and wriggle when they are trying to let us know that they are overwhelmed and need a break.

Creative relaxation (Regulation and Relaxation)

Enjoy the creative relaxation together.

HINT: Deliver script in a calm voice and at a gentle pace, with music on in the background.

Try this at home (Head, Heart and Hands)

Ask parents to practice watching their baby for a few minutes each day – next week we can catch up and see how we got on – take photos on our phones and add captions of what we think our baby is thinking – guessing is good!

Brief recap of to the session, and see you next time (Headspace and Containment)

Just recap gently what we have covered today and thank parents for coming and taking the time out of their busy days. End with goodbyes/see you next week for session 3.

"baby bonding: Week 3"
"What is attachment?"

Welcome (Headspace and Containment)

Invite parents/carers and babies to come and sit with you in a circle; name badges for parent and baby.

Welcome everyone and thank them for coming.

The hello song.

Group agreement (Headspace and Containment)

Still working OK? Stick it up on the wall.

Circle time (Headspace and Containment)

Three or four rhymes and songs to enjoy together.

HINT: Model the rhymes/songs very sensitively with your own baby, asking the baby's permission and responding to her wishes and preferences.

Breathing and regulation (Regulation and Relaxation)

Ask the group to stand in a circle; invite parents to take some deep breaths in and out; now place feet hip-width apart and feel really grounded. Gently rock from side to side, noticing when you cross the centre point. Share with parents that babies cannot regulate their own feelings and need our help – they need to borrow us when we are feeling very tired from caring for a little one! Practising centring, breathing and a gentle sway can help us feel calm and in turn calm our babies.

Watching and wondering (Head, Heart and Hands)

Ask parents to either hold their baby or lay her down – whatever they think their baby needs right now. Ask them to spend time just watching their baby – *really* watching them. This week we are going to move from our heads to our hearts. See if you can imagine what your baby is feeling right now. Guessing is good.

You can also use the guided observation questioning technique: Behaviour, Meaning, Feeling (BMF), if this supports RF more effectively:

> *Behaviour*: Let's really watch our little one and notice every tiny thing she does – breathing, twitching, blinking, flicking of fingers, a hiccup.
>
> *Meaning*: What does this behaviour mean? What is behind it?
>
> *Feeling*: What feeling is this behaviour trying to communicate?

HINT: Quiet, calm music; model carefully with your own baby – notice what is happening in the group and reflect gently. For example, "You saw that Ben was getting frustrated then – you picked up on it". Give the babies a voice, e.g. "Ben, Mummy was right about you not being happy about that; she's really trying to tune in to you".

Loving touch (Head, Heart and Hands)

Invite parents to place their baby in front of them and then to ask the baby for permission to try some loving baby touch.

Place both hands on your baby's chest and take some lovely deep breaths; practise baby strokes – add a few more; if appropriate, hum or sing "Twinkle, Twinkle, Little Star" as a loving lullaby.

HINT: Model carefully – music still on in the background.

A "gift" or "Bag of Ideas": sharing ideas and information with parents and carers (Developmental knowledge)

Share the main message that secure attachment is linked to the best outcomes for our babies and children. Share that our babies feel safe and secure when we hold them in mind, think about things from their point of view and do and say things which make them feel that we understand them. This is why we practise HHH in baby bonding; head for thoughts, heart for feelings and hands for actions and words. Give out the HHH cards for parents and carers to keep.

Handout: attachment information for parents and carers (online).

Creative relaxation (Regulation and Relaxation)

Enjoy creative relaxation together (see suggested scripts at the back of the book).

HINT: Deliver script in a calm voice and at a gentle pace, with music on in the background.

Try this at home (Head, Heart and Hands)

Ask parents to practise HHH at home with their baby, whether born or still growing inside. Encourage parents to chat to their baby: "I can see you are not happy, are you? I'll try and comfort you. Let me know if I get it wrong and I'll try something else."

Brief recap of the session and see you next time (Headspace and Containment)

Recap gently what we have covered today and thank parents for coming and taking the time out of their busy days. End with good byes/see you next time for session 4.

"baby bonding": Week 4
"Looking after me, looking after you"

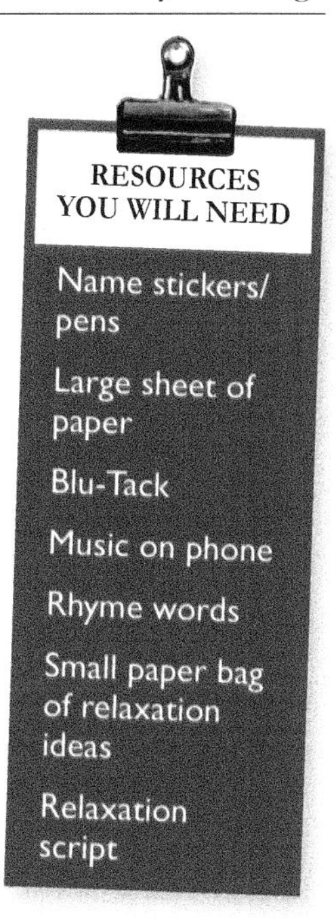

Welcome (Headspace and Containment)

Invite parents/carers and babies to come and sit with you in a circle; name badges for parent and baby.

Welcome everyone and thank them for coming.

Sing hello song.

Group agreement (Headspace and Containment)

A quick reminder.

Circle time (Headspace and Containment)

Rhymes, songs and action games (e.g. "The Wheels on the Bus", "If You're Happy and You Know It", "Wind the Bobbin Up", and others according to culture and context).

HINT: Model the rhyme very sensitively with your own baby, asking the baby's permission and responding to her wishes and preferences.

Breathing and regulation (Regulation and Relaxation)

We are going to try something different this week – baby karaoke! Practise standing up with your little one and imagine that she is unsettled and crying. Feel really grounded into the floor and take some deep breaths. Take time to settle yourself. Now think of a tune you like – maybe a pop song or another tune you know. Explain that we will match our baby's emotional "volume" with the song – as you hum or sing, walk around in time. Now slow it down a little and slow your movements, slow it again and again, nice and slowly. Finally, your tune has turned into a lullaby; gently rock from side to side, nice and calm. Baby karaoke will often help calm our babies (probably not if they are hysterical or running a temperature – but still worth a try to see if we can help them calm down and regulate).

Watching and wondering (Head, Heart and Hands)

Ask parents to practise heads and hearts – try babywatching for a few minutes to really tune in to your baby. Now try to say something to her to communicate your understanding or do something with your hands or face that responds to her needs – for example, rubbing them or a smile and nod – "I get what you need". Or rubbing our growing baby inside and asking "How are you doing in there?"

HINT: *Quiet, calm music; model carefully with your own baby. Notice what is happening in the group and reflect gently.*

Loving touch (Head, Heart and Hands)

Invite parents to place their baby in front of them and then to ask the baby for permission to try some loving baby touch. Four or five baby strokes – encourage parents/carers to hum gently to their baby, or sing "Twinkle, Twinkle" or similar as a gentle lullaby.

HINT: *Model carefully – music still on in the background.*

A "gift" or "Bag of Ideas": sharing ideas and information with parents and carers (Developmental knowledge)

A small bag filled with something to represent the need for parents to care for themselves in order to be able to care for a little one. For example, a scented candle, a bubble bath with the message "looking after me, looking after you", a sachet of hot chocolate, etc.

Creative relaxation (Regulation and Relaxation)

Enjoy together.

HINT: *Deliver script in a calm voice and at a gentle pace, with music on in the background.*

Try this at home (Head, Heart and Hands)

Ask parents to practise HHH and to make sure that they get their five minutes every day to look after themselves; add that you will check up on them next week!

Brief recap of the session and see you next time (Headspace and Containment)

Just recap gently what we have covered today; thank parents for coming and taking the time out of their busy days. End with goodbyes/see you next time – two sessions to go!

"baby bonding": Week 5
"The amazing baby brain!"

RESOURCES YOU WILL NEED

- Name stickers/pens
- Large sheet of paper
- Blu-Tack
- Music on phone
- Rhyme/song words
- Brain DVD clip
- Baby brain handout
- Coloured wool
- Relaxation script

Welcome (Headspace and Containment)

Invite parents/carers and babies to come and sit with you in a circle; name badges for parent and baby.

Welcome everyone and thank them for coming.

Sing hello song.

Group agreement (Headspace and Containment)

Quick reminder.

Circle time (Headspace and Containment)

Three or four rhymes, songs and action games as appropriate.

HINT: Model the rhyme very sensitively with your own baby, asking the baby's permission and responding to her wishes and preferences.

Breathing and regulation (Regulation and Relaxation)

Repeat baby karaoke from last week. Did anyone have a chance to try it at home – did it help? Not to worry if it didn't – it's a technique to try sometimes.

Watching and wondering (Head, Heart and Hands)

Ask parents to either hold their baby or lay her down – whatever they think their baby needs right now.

Practise heads

Practise hearts

Practise hands

Doing this helps our baby feel safe and secure – research shows that HHH helps support secure attachment.

HINT: Quiet, calm music; model carefully with your own baby. Gently notice and reflect what you see between parent and baby – also giving the babies a voice in this process.

Loving touch (Head, Heart and Hands)

Invite parents to place their baby in front of them and then to ask the baby for permission to try some loving baby touch.

Baby strokes – practise favourite ones together – respond to the babies.

HINT: Model carefully – music still on in the background.

A "gift" or "Bag of Ideas": sharing ideas and information with parents and carers (Developmental knowledge)

Enjoy watching a clip about the amazing baby brain (links online to several suggested videos).

Handout: Colourful information about our baby's brain development and how we can help support it through simple everyday activities.

Play the "wool game". In the circle, hold a small ball of wool – each parent is a neuron (brain cell). The practitioner goes first and says that singing to our baby helps build her brain, then passes the ball to a parent across the circle whilst keeping hold of the end – this parent then comes up with another idea for building a brain, for example chatting and listening during nappy-changing. This parent keeps hold of the wool and passes the ball to another parent. Keep going until you have a "web" of wool across the circle. Use this to illustrate to parents how these simple things are creating the grey matter of your baby's brain. You help to wire her brain! Babies usually enjoy being under the woollen web and will often grab at it. Or parents can adjust their baby's position sensitively.

Creative relaxation (Regulation and Relaxation)

Enjoy together.

HINT: Deliver script in a calm voice and at a gentle pace, with music on in the background.

Try this at home (Head, Heart and Hands)

Ask parents to practise HHH and to enjoy noticing how they are helping their baby's brain development through everyday activities.

Brief recap of the session and see you next time (Headspace and Containment)

Recap gently what we have covered today and thank parents for coming and taking the time out of their busy days. End with good byes/see you next time for our final session.

"baby bonding": Week 6 "'baby bonding' celebrations"

RESOURCES YOU WILL NEED

- Name stickers/pens
- Group agreement
- Blu-Tack
- Music on phone
- Rhyme words
- Songbook
- Cake/fruit
- Relaxation script
- Certificates
- Evaluation forms
- Story book
- Information on other services and groups

Welcome (Headspace and Containment)

Invite parents/carers and babies to come and sit with you in a circle; name badges for parent and baby.

Welcome everyone and thank them for coming.

Sing hello song.

Group agreement (Headspace and Containment)

Thank everyone for being such a respectful and supportive group.

Circle time (Headspace and Containment)

Enjoy our favourite rhymes and songs; give out a little book of songs chosen by the group. Include multicultural songs that represent the heritage of the group.

HINT: Model the rhyme very sensitively with your own baby, asking the baby's permission and responding to her wishes and preferences.

Breathing and regulation (Regulation and Relaxation)

Conducted breathing for our last session together: breathe in for the count of 3, hold for 3 and breath out for 3 – practise once. Then increase to count of 6, then 9, then 12 – have fun with this. I count for the group "in–2–3, hold–2–3, out–2–3".

Watching and wondering (Head, Heart and Hands)

Our final practice at HHH – congratulate the group on their progress in this. Encourage parents and carers to continue to use this technique as their children grow.

Loving touch (Head, Heart and Hands)

Enjoy our favourite baby strokes together; encourage parents to continue with these each day when their baby is in the mood.

HINT: Model carefully – music still on in the background.

A "gift" or "Bag of Ideas": sharing ideas and information with parents and carers (Developmental knowledge)

Read a lovely story, poem or song words to parents and babies – something affirming and uplifting. I like Emma Dodd's animal books, which are written in the voice of the baby and transcend family stereotypes (see, for example, *Forever*). Enjoy sharing some cake and fruit together.

Creative relaxation (Regulation and Relaxation)

Enjoy this together. Again, encourage parents to continue relaxing each day and tell them that if they are OK then they are much better able to look after their baby.

Try this at home (Head, Heart and Hands)

Ask parents to continue practising HHH.

Brief recap of the session and goodbyes (Headspace and Containment)

Thank parents for coming to the group and for all their input and efforts.

Ask parents to complete a short evaluation and to share their thoughts about the group.

Present baby bonding certificates.

Provide any relevant information about follow-on groups or services.

Goodbyes.

Appendix 2

A programme for parents, carers and toddlers

Six sample sessions

"toddler bonding": Week 1
"Welcome to 'toddler bonding'"

RESOURCES YOU WILL NEED

- Name stickers/pens
- Group agreement
- Blu-Tack
- Music on phone
- Rhyme words
- Everyday treasure box (shoe box)
- Pieces of fabric
- Bangles, ribbon, wool etc.
- Stretchy ring
- Toddler handout
- Relaxation script

Welcome (Headspace and Containment)

Invite parents/carers and toddlers to come and sit with you in a circle; parents/carers make name badges for themselves and toddler. Welcome everyone and thank them for coming. Sing the hello song (your own or from online resources). Have a small everyday treasure box available for toddlers to enjoy – they might potter about or sit with their parent/carer. Treasure box contains everyday items such as a brush, sponge, home-made shaker, scarf, pine cone, shell, boxes to stack, etc.

Over the next weeks together we will be learning about the latest findings from attachment research and trying out ideas with our own little ones. If your toddler is not actually in the mood for our activities, it's OK – the best stuff happens at home! We also have our "spare" babies to practise on during the session.

Group agreement (Headspace and Containment)

Invite parents to help you write a short list of things that will help the group go well and be a safe place for all. Examples: mobiles on silent, respect each other, listen to each other, what we say in this room stays in this room, etc.

For toddlers it is vital to include that parents and carers must look after their child at *all* times; if their child potters about, the parents must be with them. The parent is responsible for their child, not the practitioner.

Circle time (Headspace and Containment)

Gently introduce the toddler bonding session structure: we begin with a few simple rhymes, songs or activities each week. Start with repeating a familiar and appropriate rhyme with actions; ask parents to watch their toddler to see what she likes or if she enjoys the actions; encourage them to change in response to their toddler's wishes, e.g. "The Grand Old Duke of York".

HINT: Model the rhyme very sensitively with your baby, asking permission and responding to her wishes and preferences.

HINT: Use a few pairs of old children's striped or patterned tights tied together to make a stretchy ring – this can help contain toddlers and encourage their curiosity! I sometimes tie extra things onto the stretchy ring to make it multi-sensory, for example men's ties, scarves in see-through fabrics, plastic strips that rustle, etc.

Breathing and regulation (Regulation and Relaxation)

Explain that we understand that being a parent of a toddler is very hard and tiring. Also acknowledge to toddlers that you understand that it can be very hard and tiring being a toddler. Invite the group to take some deep breaths in and out and gently share how important it is that we take time to breathe when things are tough. Practise together for a few minutes. Toddlers will often copy and join in!

HINT: It can help to keep the stretchy ring for this activity.

Watching and wondering (Head, Heart and Hands)

Ask parents to offer their toddler a piece of fabric from the fabric bag (fabric pieces, tea towels, scarves, hankies, etc.). Parents take one too, but focus more on their toddler. Ask parents to watch their toddler playing with the fabric very carefully. If toddlers invite their parent into their play, parents respond, being careful not to take over. Notice if you start thinking about other things! Come back to your toddler and practise. Explain that research shows that parents who spend time really watching and thinking about their babies begin to understand their signals better and feel more of an expert in their own child. Ask parents to practice heads – try toddler-watching for a few minutes to really tune in to your toddler.

HINT: Quiet, calm music; model carefully with your own baby. Notice what is happening in the group and reflect gently. Give the toddlers a voice, e.g. "You liked your Mummy doing that, Nia – she felt how much you needed that cuddle".

Loving touch (Head, Heart and Hands)

Invite parents to ask their toddler for permission to try some loving toddler touch. Offer spare babies to parents whose toddlers are not interested at this time. Place both hands on your toddler's chest and take some lovely deep breaths – imagine that you are sending your breath into your toddler. Practise the "velvet cloak" baby stroke or another simple baby stroke (see online resources).

HINT: Model carefully with your own baby – music still on in the background.

A "gift" or "Bag of Ideas": sharing ideas and information with parents and carers (Developmental knowledge)

Each week, we share a gift with parents or an idea – something to nurture parents, carers and toddlers. We also share important information about toddler development. Invite parents and toddlers to pick out a solid bangle/curtain ring from a selection you have brought: one for the parent, one for the toddler. Uninterested toddlers can potter around – everyday treasure is available for them to explore. Offer a selection of recycled ribbons, wool, lace trim, etc., to tie to the bangle to make a lovely streamer toy. Whilst enjoying making these, explain that attachment theory is really clear – toddlers need us to be good enough and not perfect! – rather like this bangle, which is home-made and personal. Our toddlers enjoy quality time with us and enjoy everyday "treasure". Enjoy chatting this through if parents want to discuss. Emphasise that, for safety, parents need to supervise their children with everyday items. Small children must not be left alone with home-made toys.

Handout: Attractive information sheet on toddler development; be sensitive to literacy/language etc. and adapt as needed (see online resources).

Creative relaxation (Regulation and Relaxation)

Ask parents/carers and toddlers to make themselves comfortable. If toddlers are pottering about, offer to watch over them during the relaxation exercise. (Remind group that the practitioner can watch over the toddlers, but the parents remain responsible.) Enjoy relaxing together.

HINT: Deliver script in a calm voice and at a gentle pace, with quiet music on.

Try this at home (Head, Heart and Hands)

Ask parents to practise watching their toddler for a few minutes each day; ask them to start by carefully watching what she is doing and see if they can guess what she is thinking. Next week we can see how everyone got on. "Don't worry if you find it difficult – it is hard, especially with all the demands of being a parent."

Brief recap of the session and see you next time (Headspace and Containment)

Recap gently what we have covered today and thank parents for coming and taking the time out of their busy days. End with goodbyes and see you all next time for Week 2.

"toddler bonding": Week 2
"I'm OK, you're OK"

RESOURCES YOU WILL NEED

- Name stickers/pens
- Group agreement
- Blu-Tack
- Music on phone
- Rhyme words
- Stretchy ring
- Everyday treasure box
- Everyday instruments
- "Time for me" bags
- Relaxation script

Welcome (Headspace and Containment)

Invite parents/carers and toddlers to come and sit with you in a circle; name badges for parent/carer and toddler. Welcome everyone and thank them for coming. Sing the hello song; everyday treasure. How did we get on toddler-watching since last week? How easy or difficult is it to hold your child in mind? Discussion may follow.

Group agreement (Headspace and Containment)

Gentle reminder: is it working OK for us? Anything to add?

Circle time (Headspace and Containment)

Repeat rhymes from last week. Ask parents to watch their toddler to see what they like or if they enjoy the actions. Encourage them to change in response to their toddler's wishes; add new rhymes and songs with actions.

HINT: Model the rhyme very sensitively with your baby, asking permission and responding to her wishes and preferences.

Breathing and regulation (Regulation and Relaxation)

Practise deep breathing together for a few minutes – feel the breath deep into our bodies. The stretchy ring can be stretched out for breaths in and come back to normal on breaths out – vary as appropriate.

Watching and wondering (Head, Heart and Hands)

Ask parents to offer their toddler an everyday instrument from the instrument bag (home-made shakers, pan lids, wooden spoons, etc.). Parents take one too, but focus more on their toddler. Ask parents to watch their toddler closely. If toddlers invite their parent into their play, parents respond, being careful not to take over. Notice if you start thinking about other things!

HINT: Quiet, calm music; model carefully with your own baby. Notice what is happening in the group and reflect gently. Give toddlers a voice, e.g. "Billy, you love that sound, I can see!"

Loving touch (Head, Heart and Hands)

Invite parents to ask their toddler for permission to try some loving toddler touch. Offer spare babies to parents whose toddlers are not interested at this time. Deep breathing and "velvet cloak" – add two or three new strokes.

HINT: Model carefully – music still on in the background.

A "gift" or "Bag of Ideas": sharing ideas and information with parents and carers (Developmental knowledge)

"Time for me": Offer parents and carers a small bag containing something to encourage them to make some time for themselves to rest. Ideas: sachet of hot chocolate, bubble bath bomb, plus a small card with affirming message or quote.

Creative relaxation (Regulation and Relaxation)

Enjoy together.

HINT: Deliver script in a calm voice and at a gentle pace, with quiet music on.

Try this at home (Head, Heart and Hands)

Ask parents to practise watching their toddler for a few minutes each day. Ask them to start by carefully watching what she is doing and see if they can guess what she is thinking. Why does she do what she does? Become a detective in thinking about your toddler's thinking. We'll catch up on this next week.

Brief recap of the session and see you next time (Headspace and Containment)

Just recap gently what we have covered today and thank parents for coming and taking the time out of their busy days. End with goodbyes/see you next week for our third session.

"toddler bonding": Week 3
"Brain change: tots and tantrums"

RESOURCES YOU WILL NEED

- Name stickers/pens
- Group agreement
- Blu-Tack
- Music on phone
- Rhyme words
- Everyday treasure box
- Mini sensory shakers
- Stretchy ring
- Brain quiz
- Toddler's brain handout
- "Guessing is good" cards
- Relaxation script

Welcome (Headspace and Containment)

Invite parents/carers and toddlers to come and sit with you in a circle; name badges for parent/carer and toddler. Welcome everyone and thank them for coming.

Sing the hello song – everyday treasure.

Group agreement (Headspace and Containment)

Gentle reminder; is it working OK for us? Anything to add?

Circle time (Headspace and Containment)

Repeat rhymes and songs; add new ones – ask the group for ones they remember from their childhood. Maybe one of the group has rhymes and songs in another language. Perhaps this parent can teach us these and help us write them down – in normal script and, alongside, in phonetics to help pronunciation.

HINT: Model the rhyme very sensitively with your baby, asking her permission and responding to her wishes and preferences.

Breathing and regulation (Regulation and Relaxation)

Practise deep breathing together for a few minutes; try standing up with feet hip-width apart – feel grounded and centred. Use the stretchy ring – lift it up on the breath in, and bring it back down on the breath out.

Watching and wondering (Head, Heart and Hands)

Ask parents to offer their toddler a mini sensory shaker from the bag (small recycled bottles filled with water and either glitter, rubber bands, paper clips, buttons or sequins – lids *must* be taped or glued on!) Parents take one too, but focus more on their toddler. Ask parents to watch their toddler very closely. Think about her – what is she thinking? Feel her feelings. If toddlers invite their parent into their play, parents respond, being careful not to take over. Notice if you start thinking about other things!

HINT: Quiet, calm music; model carefully with your own baby. Notice what is happening in the group and reflect gently. Give toddlers a voice too.

HINT: Can use alternative scaffolding for RF with the BMF technique.

Loving touch (Head, Heart and Hands)

Invite parents to ask their toddler for permission to try some loving toddler touch. Offer spare babies to parents whose toddlers are not interested at this time. Practise strokes and add new ones.

HINT: Model carefully – music on in the background.

A "gift" or "Bag of Ideas": sharing ideas and information with parents and carers (Developmental knowledge)

Share fun information with parents and carers about what is happening in their toddler's brain and how that can make her seem "difficult". Play the brain quiz and hand out the fun sheet for parents/carers (see online resources for video links, quiz and sample handouts).

Creative relaxation (Regulation and Relaxation)

Enjoy together.

HINT: Deliver script in a calm voice and at a gentle pace, with quiet music on.

Try this at home (Head, Heart and Hands)

Ask parents to practise thinking about their toddler (heads) and really entering into their feelings with them (hearts), even if those feelings are hard. Practise letting your toddler know that you know she is happy/frustrated/annoyed/tired, etc. – have a guess and let her know!

Give out "Guessing is good" card – just the right size to stick on the fridge or keep in a purse or wallet.

Brief recap of the session and see you next time (Headspace and Containment)

A gentle recap of what we have covered today and thank parents for coming and taking the time out of their busy days. End with goodbyes and see you next week for session 4.

"toddler bonding": Week 4
"Why does attachment matter?"

RESOURCES YOU WILL NEED

- Name stickers/pens
- Group agreement
- Blu-Tack
- Music on phone
- Rhyme words
- Everyday treasure box
- "Did you know?" quiz
- Attachment handout
- Attachment video clip
- Relaxation script

Welcome (Headspace and Containment)

Invite parents/carers and toddlers to come and sit with you in a circle; name badges for parent/carer and toddler. Welcome everyone and thank them for coming.

Sing the hello song; everyday treasure. How did we get on recognising and reflecting on our toddlers' thoughts and feelings since last week? Any good guesses?

Group agreement (Headspace and Containment)

Gentle reminder; is it working OK for us? Anything to add?

Circle time (Headspace and Containment)

Rhymes, songs and action games – have fun.

HINT: Model the rhyme very sensitively with your baby, asking permission and responding to her wishes and preferences.

Breathing and regulation (Regulation and Relaxation)

Practise deep breathing together for a few minutes. Try standing up with feet hip-width apart; feel grounded and centred. Hum a familiar tune together – anything from a pop song to a TV advert theme – and sway in time.

Watching and wondering (Head, Heart and Hands)

Toddlers choose from the everyday treasure whilst parents just think (heads), feel (hearts) and now try to do or say something that lets their child know that she is understood. A nod, a word or two, a rub on the back – anything that lets the child know that her parent is trying to understand her. This can be verbal and/or non-verbal.

HINT: Quiet, calm music; model carefully with your own baby. Notice what is happening in the group and reflect gently. Give the toddlers a voice in this process. Help parents gain insight into what might be happening for their toddler. Guessing is good!

Loving touch (Head, Heart and Hands)

Invite parents to ask their toddler for permission to try some loving toddler touch. Offer spare babies to parents whose toddlers are not interested at this time. Practise and add additional strokes as appropriate.

HINT: Model carefully, with music still on in the background.

A "gift" or "Bag of Ideas": sharing ideas and information with parents and carers (Developmental knowledge)

Share attachment information with parents, including handout on how parents can support toddlers. Enjoy the "Did you know?" quiz and video on attachment. (Attachment information for parents, the quiz, and video links are available online).

Creative relaxation (Regulation and Relaxation)

Enjoy together.

HINT: Deliver script in a calm voice and at a gentle pace, with quiet music on.

Try this at home (Head, Heart and Hands)

Ask parents to practise HHH at home in the coming week. Make time every day to toddler-watch; think about her, wonder what she is thinking and feeling and let her know that you understand her – with a word or an action.

Brief recap of the session and see you next time (Headspace and Containment)

Just recap gently on what we have covered today and thank parents for coming and taking the time out of their busy days. End with goodbyes and see you next time for session 5. Two weeks to go!

"toddler bonding": Week 5 "Catch them making helpful choices"

Welcome (Headspace and Containment)

Invite parents/carers and toddlers to come and sit with you in a circle; name badges for parent/carer and toddler. Welcome everyone and thank them for coming.

Sing the hello song; everyday treasure available. How is HHH going at home?

Group agreement (Headspace and Containment)

Gentle reminder; is it working OK for us? Anything to add?

Circle time (Headspace and Containment)

Rhymes, songs and action games.

HINT: Model the rhyme very sensitively with your baby, asking permission and responding to her wishes and preferences.

Breathing and regulation (Regulation and Relaxation)

Practise deep breathing together for a few minutes. Offer parents and toddlers a beautiful sheet to colour in mindfully and to help regulation (links available online).

Watching and wondering (Head, Heart and Hands)

Offer a king-size duvet cover or sheet to be held by the parents and carers for the toddlers to enjoy going underneath with their legs in the air, etc. Parents billow up the duvet cover/sheet and then bring it down – this is effectively a home-made parachute. Watch our children and practise HHH. See online resource bank for more parachute games to try.

HINT: Quiet, calm music; model carefully with your own baby. Notice what is happening in the group and reflect gently.

Loving touch (Head, Heart and Hands)

Invite parents to ask their toddler for permission to try some loving toddler touch. Enjoy favourite strokes together.

HINT: Model sensitively, with music still on in the background.

A "gift" or "Bag of Ideas": sharing ideas and information with parents and carers (Developmental knowledge)

Share with parents ideas from research about how to encourage toddlers to make helpful choices. Play the Marshmallow Test clip on YouTube, which shows parents just how amazing their children can be when faced with temptation; this leads to a lovely discussion about how positive children's behaviour can be.

Handout: 15 things to help children's behaviour choices become more helpful (video links and handout available online).

Creative relaxation (Regulation and Relaxation)

Enjoy together.

HINT: Deliver script in a calm voice and at a gentle pace, with quiet music on.

Try this at home (Head, Heart and Hands)

Ask parents to practise HHH at home every day.

Brief recap of the session and see you next time (Headspace and Containment)

Recap gently what we have covered today and thank parents for coming and taking the time out of their busy days. End with goodbyes and see you next week for our final session together.

"toddler bonding": Week 6 "Time to celebrate"

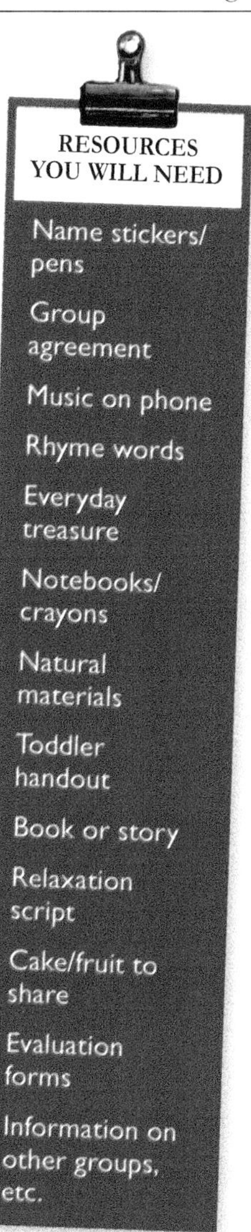

Welcome (Headspace and Containment)

Invite parents/carers and toddlers to come and sit with you in a circle; name badges for parent/carer and toddler. Welcome everyone and thank them for coming.

Sing the hello song; everyday treasure available.

Group agreement (Headspace and Containment)

Thank you for helping to make this group a safe and respectful place for all parents/carers and toddlers.

Mention that the idea of a group agreement can be used at home once the children are about three years old. The whole family can agree together just a few rules which everyone keeps. When the rules are broken, an age-appropriate and non-punitive agreed consequence takes place. The whole family works on making choices within the boundary of non-punitive but predictable consequences. Parents and carers model the rules, keep the boundaries and also apologise when they get it wrong.

Circle time (Headspace and Containment)

Favourite rhymes and songs. Give out a home-made songbook of the group's favourites (the group could also help to make this).

Breathing and regulation (Regulation and Relaxation)

Offer paper and nice notebooks and a bundle of coloured pencils/crayons to parents/carers and toddlers, perhaps with a positive message on the front. Encourage parents to take time relaxing and focusing on their breathing each day and to use these doodle books.

Watching and wondering (Head, Heart and Hands)

Toddlers choose from a selection of natural objects (pine cones, leaves, shells, lavender, conkers, etc.). Toddlers will usually explore these natural objects without prompting. Time to practise HHH: a nod, a word or two, a rub on the back – anything that lets the child know that her parent is trying to understand her.

HINT: Quiet, calm music; model carefully with your own baby. Notice what is happening in the group and reflect gently.

Loving touch (Head, Heart and Hands)

Invite parents to ask their toddler for permission to try some loving toddler touch. Enjoy favourite strokes together.

HINT: Model carefully, with music still on in the background.

A "gift" or "Bag of Ideas": sharing ideas and information with parents and carers (Developmental knowledge)

Share an attractive book with the group. My favourite is Emma Dodd's *Me* (Templar Publishing, 2010), but of course there are other lovely stories. Choose an uplifting one for your final session together.

Creative relaxation (Regulation and Relaxation)

Enjoy together.

HINT: Deliver script in a calm voice and at a gentle pace, with quiet music on.

Try this at home (Head, Heart and Hands)

Continue finding just a couple of minutes every day to practise HHH – let it become part of family life. Also practise on your wider family and friends and notice how relationships become more secure.

Brief recap and goodbyes (Headspace and Containment)

Just recap gently what we have covered over the weeks.

Evaluation and presentation of certificates; enjoy cake/fruit together.

Give parents/carers ideas for other groups and services that may continue to support them going forward.

Goodbyes.

Appendix 3

A programme for parents, carers and their children and teenagers

Six sample sessions for five- to nine-year-olds*

* approximate age group

H2H 5 to 9 years: Week 1 "Welcome to H2H"

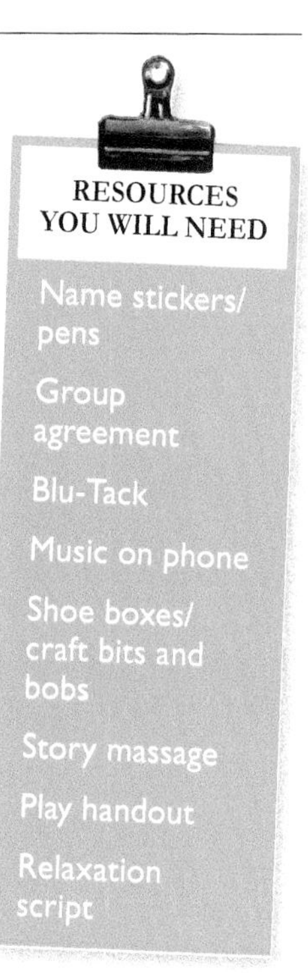

Welcome (Headspace and Containment)

Invite parents/carers and children to come and sit with you in a circle; make name badges together.

Welcome everyone and thank them for coming.

Sing the hello song (your own or from online resource bank).

Group agreement (Headspace and Containment)

Invite parents and children to help you write a short list of things that will help the group go well and be a safe place for all. Examples: mobiles on silent, respect for each other, listen to each other, our choice how to join in – always ensure that children's voices are included in this exercise.

Circle time (Headspace and Containment)

Gently introduce the session structure; each week we begin with a few simple games, songs or activities.

Our names: give everyone a sheet of paper and pens to make a poster all about them – their name, things they like, etc. If practicable, laminating these will make them look great. Share your own name's meaning or similar, then invite parents and children to share their posters – where their name comes from, what it means, things they like, etc. NB: volunteers only.

HINT: Model carefully, offering children a choice of colours and paper. Ask parents to acknowledge their child's preferences and only to help or contribute if invited to by their child.

Breathing and regulation (Regulation and Relaxation)

Explain that being a parent and being a child is sometimes very hard. Invite parents, carers and children to take some deep breaths in and out and gently share how important it is that we take time to breathe when things are tough. Practise together for a few minutes.

Watching and wondering (Head, Heart and Hands)

Offer each pair a choice of shoe boxes filled with some craft bits and bobs – paper, pens, recycled bits, whatever is appropriate, plus a small roll of sticky tape. Invite children to explore the box and see what's inside for a few minutes. Ask parents and carers to sit alongside their child and really focus on them. Notice if you start thinking about other things! Come back to your child and practise. Explain that research shows that parents who spend time really watching and thinking about their children begin to understand them better and feel more of an expert in their own child. This is linked to strengthening relationships. Of course, the children are also hearing this gentle explanation as they play. Ensure that there is one extra box so that all pairs have a real choice.

HINT: Quiet, gentle music playing on a phone or Bluetooth speaker.

NB: This is the start of us focusing on RF. We take slow steps week by week.

Loving touch (Head, Heart and Hands)

Invite parents and children to sit in a circle again, this time all facing in one direction. Invite them to join in a fun story – which we will tell on each other's backs! NB: Everyone must ask the person in front of them for permission to touch them – also remind everyone about the group agreement. Use the cooking massage story (script online) or make up your own.

Alternative activity: Again sitting in a circle all facing one way, after asking permission from the person in front, draw shapes on their back using your finger with gentle but firm pressure. This can be extended to ask them to draw animals, etc.

A "gift" or "Bag of Ideas": sharing ideas and information with parents and carers (Developmental knowledge)

Each week, we share a gift or an idea with parents – something to nurture parents and children and also share important information about child development.

Invite parents and children to take their shoebox home. Encourage parents and carers to help children keep it safe and to enjoy playing with it. Card for parents and carers – "I am my child's favourite playmate!" Encourage parents to believe that, despite everything, they are indeed a favourite playmate!

Handout: Attractive information sheet on play and how important it is for our children's development; be sensitive to literacy/language (use online resource bank).

Creative relaxation (Regulation and Relaxation)

Explain that each week we enjoy creative relaxation together; invite the group to join in and enjoy some peaceful and relaxing time (sample scripts in online resource bank). Read the story in a calm voice with a nice unhurried pace, with music in the background.

Try this at home (Head, Heart and Hands)

Ask parents to practise playing with their child for a few minutes each day. Ask them to start by carefully watching what she is doing and see if they can guess what she is thinking. Next week, the group can catch up and see how we got on; tell parents not to worry if they find it hard – it *is* hard, especially with all the demands of being a parent!

Brief recap of the session and see you next time (Headspace and Containment)

Just recap gently what we have covered today and thank parents and children for coming and taking the time out of their busy days. End with goodbyes and see you next week for session 2.

H2H 5 to 9 years: Week 2 "Mind-reading!"

Welcome (Headspace and Containment)

Invite parents/carers and children to come and sit with you in a circle; make name badges together.

Welcome everyone and thank them for coming.

Sing the hello song. How did our shoebox playtimes at home go?

Group agreement (Headspace and Containment)

Is this working OK? Anything to add?

Circle time (Headspace and Containment)

Stretch out the stretchy ring (I use old pairs of striped tights tied together, but you could use old ties or pieces of cord or ribbon, even plastic bags – everyday things, nothing special). The ring joins everyone together without forcing the holding of hands. Enjoy a couple of action songs together – "The Hokey Cokey" is a favourite in the UK – or songs in a second language, or a favourite pop tune.

Breathing and regulation (Regulation and Relaxation)

Keep hold of the stretchy ring; explain that being a parent and being a child is sometimes very hard. Invite parents, carers and children to take some deep breaths in and out and gently share how important it is that we take time to breathe when things are tough. Practise together for a few minutes. The ring made of tights is handy for this because the group can stretch it out on breathing in and release on breathing out.

Watching and wondering (Head, Heart and Hands)

Invite parents and carers and children to play a guessing game together whilst facing each other. Model it first with a co-practitioner or a parent/carer volunteer (NB: not with a child).

Parent or carer thinks of an animal and the child has to guess what the animal is. At first, give no clues, and see if the child can read the adult's mind! Second, the parent/carer gives a small clue – can you [the child] guess it yet? Now give a big clue. Swap over – encourage everyone to try to mind-read.

HINT: Quiet, gentle music playing on a phone or Bluetooth speaker.

Loving touch (Head, Heart and Hands)

Invite parents and children to sit in a circle, all facing in one direction. Invite them to join in a fun story which we will tell on each other's backs. We do the story twice – once facing one way and then after turning the other. (NB: Everyone must ask the person in front of them for permission to touch them – also remind everyone about the group agreement.)

Use the weather massage story or your own (see stories in online resource bank).

A "gift" or "Bag of Ideas": sharing ideas and information with parents and carers (Developmental knowledge)

Explain that all of us – parents/carers and children – need time to chill out and relax. Hand out postcards with "Time for me" printed on – have a box of pens, stickers, etc. to decorate. Now invite everyone to take these home and make time to rest and relax before next week's session – especially parents and carers, who are responsible for looking after everyone in the family.

Creative relaxation (Regulation and Relaxation)

Enjoy the creative relaxation together – invite the group to join in and enjoy some peaceful and relaxing time.

Try this at home (Head, Heart and Hands)

Ask parents/carers and children to play the animal guessing game, or another game they like, together in the coming week – practise mind-reading! Next week we can catch up and see how we got on. Shoebox play can be continued at home.

Brief recap of the session and see you next time (Headspace and Containment)

Just recap gently what we have covered today and thank parents and children for coming and taking the time out of their busy days. End with goodbyes and see you next week for session 3.

H2H 5 to 9 years: Week 3 "You and me together"

Welcome (Headspace and Containment)

Invite parents/carers and children to come and sit with you in a circle; make name badges together.

Welcome everyone and thank them for coming.

Sing the hello song. How did the guessing games go at home?

Group agreement (Headspace and Containment)

Is this working OK? Anything to add?

Circle time (Headspace and Containment)

Stretch out the stretchy ring; do some action songs (ideas online).

Breathing and regulation (Regulation and Relaxation)

Practise breathing in and out a few times – nice and deeply.

Next, lift the ring up on breathing in and stretch up on your toes as high as you can. Breathe out and slowly crouch down to the floor. Practise together for a few minutes.

Watching and wondering (Head, Heart and Hands)

Invite parents and carers and children to make "You and me together" artwork. Model it first with your co-practitioner or a volunteer parent/carer.

Each child makes one squiggle on a piece of paper with a crayon/ pen. Parent adds another, joined to it. Child adds again, then parent; they keep going to make their own piece of squiggle art together. No talking is allowed! Ask them to both "sign" their "you and me" art (this can be laminated if desired). Ask parents/carers to really think about what their child is doing; watch her carefully and guess what she is thinking of.

HINT: *Quiet, gentle music playing on a phone or Bluetooth speaker.*

Loving touch (Head, Heart and Hands)

Circle story massage as before – once facing one way and next facing the other (permission requested both times). Animal massage story (script online), or your own.

A "gift" or "Bag of Ideas": sharing ideas and information with parents and carers (Developmental knowledge)

Offer everyone a choice of small notebooks/paper and a small bundle of crayons/pencils. Invite everyone to write their name on the front and to enjoy time to doodle, draw and be creative during the coming week.

Creative relaxation (Regulation and Relaxation)

Enjoy the creative relaxation.

Try this at home (Head, Heart and Hands)

Ask parents and children to spend a few minutes each day playing or doodling together. Parents should really focus on their child – what is she thinking, how is she feeling today? See if you can mind-read – guessing is good!

Brief recap of the session and see you next time (Headspace and Containment)

Gentle recap of what we have covered today and thank parents and children for coming and taking the time out of their busy days. End with goodbyes and see you next week for session 4.

H2H 5 to 9 years: Week 4 "Feelings"

Welcome (Headspace and Containment)

Invite parents/carers and children to come and sit with you in a circle; make name badges together.

Welcome everyone and thank them for coming.

Sing the hello song. How did we get on playing and doodling together this week?

Group agreement (Headspace and Containment)

Is this working OK? Anything to add?

Circle time (Headspace and Containment)

Stretchy ring – enjoy a few songs together.

Play "Pass the touch" game. Practitioner begins by passing a touch to the next person in the circle – who then passes it to the next person, and so on. NB: The touch must adhere to the group agreement; for example, gently tap the shoulder once, then twice on the knee. Using your foot, gently tap the next person's foot, etc. When the same touch has gone round the circle once, try a different one in the opposite direction.

Breathing and regulation (Regulation and Relaxation)

Standing in a circle, take deep breaths in and out. On breathing in stretch up, and on breathing out bend down to the floor. If appropriate, parent/carer and child can face each other and mirror this together.

Watching and wondering (Head, Heart and Hands)

Invite parents and carers and children to stand facing each other with arms straight out in front and hands pressing together to make a bridge. Push gently and see if you can balance – move feet backwards a little – press and balance – try a bit further! Enjoy and keep trying. No talking throughout these games!

Another version is to stand closely together, hold wrists and lean back – see if you can increase the lean and trust between parent and child. Parents, really watch your child and tune in to how she is feeling through your hands and the balance.

HINT: Quiet, gentle music playing on a phone or Bluetooth speaker.

Loving touch (Head, Heart and Hands)

Circle story massage, as before – once facing one way and then facing the other (permission requested both times).

Use "Going on a Bear Hunt" massage story (see online), or your own.

A "gift" or "Bag of Ideas": sharing ideas and information with parents and carers (Developmental knowledge)

Use some fun cards with babies, toddlers, children, teens and adults all showing different facial expressions. Play "guess how they are feeling" with the group (ideas online).

Give out a little card with the question "How are you feeling right now?" Ask parents and carers to put it up somewhere at home and reflect on how feelings change so much from one moment to the next.

Creative relaxation (Regulation and Relaxation)

Enjoy the creative relaxation together.

Try this at home (Head, Heart and Hands)

Ask parents and children to have a few minutes' shoebox play together each day; they can top the box up with a few extra supplies – things that the child enjoys. Parents, really focus on your child and see if you can feel her feelings as she plays.

Imagine how your child feels from her point of view. Can you say something that lets her know that she is understood, or perhaps you can use non-verbal nods and smiles or short statements like "I understand", "You want that one", etc.

Brief recap of the session and see you next time (Headspace and Containment)

Just recap gently what we have covered today and thank parents and children for coming and taking the time out of their busy days. End with goodbyes and see you next time – two sessions to go!

H2H 5 to 9 years: Week 5
"My heart, your heart"

Welcome (Headspace and Containment)

Invite parents/carers and children to come and sit with you in a circle; make name badges together.

Welcome everyone and thank them for coming.

Sing the hello song. How did feeling your child's feelings go?

Group agreement (Headspace and Containment)

Is this working OK? Anything to add?

Circle time (Headspace and Containment)

A song or two with the stretchy ring – or maybe it's OK to hold hands at this point.

Play "Pass the ball". A ball is passed around the circle without anyone using their hands! A soft ball is best for this. When one ball is going around, add another and then a third. Have fun! Adapt game if needed.

Breathing and regulation (Regulation and Relaxation)

Parent/carer and child practise deep breathing, mirroring together, for a few minutes. Gently explain to parents/carers that we help regulate our children – when the going gets tough, start to breathe. (Safeguarding message: a good enough parent will take a few minutes to compose themselves if they feel they are losing their temper).

Watching and wondering (Head, Heart and Hands)

Invite parents and carers to make a strong shape with their bodies, standing up or on the floor. Invite their child to find a way to hide "inside" this shape.

Then develop into the "monsters" game (or other appropriate name).

Parents and carers stay in their safe shapes around the room; when the music plays the children can move around the room, and when the music stops they must run back to their parent and hide in their shape (monsters are coming!). Parents, really watch your child and tune in to how she hides "inside" you and finds this comforting.

HINT: Quiet, gentle music playing on a phone or Bluetooth speaker.

Loving touch (Head, Heart and Hands)

Repeat favourite massage story so far or invite parents, carers and children to make up one of their own.

A "gift" or "Bag of Ideas": sharing ideas and information with parents and carers (Developmental knowledge)

Introduce how attachment works: it is just like the "monsters" game – children do best in life when they have a safe adult who helps them with difficult or scary feelings.

Handout: on attachment (online).

Introduce head, heart and hands card. Research has shown that practising this helps children feel safer and more secure with their parent/carer.

The BMF technique can be used if this feels more appropriate for the group.

Creative relaxation (Regulation and Relaxation)

Enjoy together; ask everyone to practise this at home – music is not essential and they can imagine your voice. Where it is possible, I have given or lent families a relaxation CD to use at home, or put music onto mobile phones to encourage relaxation time.

Try this at home (Head, Heart and Hands)

Ask parents to practise HHH whilst playing with their child for a few minutes each day. Start by carefully watching what she is doing, move onto to her thoughts and feelings, and finally try and say or do something that lets her know that you understand her. For example, a loud noise makes your child jump and you rub her back and say, "You didn't like that – it made you really jump"; make a short statement or give a non-verbal signal so your child feels understood, safe and secure in that moment. Guessing is good – our children will correct us if we are not quite right – it still makes them feel understood and connected with us.

Brief recap of the session and see you next time (Headspace and Containment)

Gently recap what we have covered today and thank parents and children for coming and taking the time out of their busy days. End with goodbyes and see you next week for our final session together.

H2H 5 to 9 years: Week 6 "Celebrations"

RESOURCES YOU WILL NEED

- Name stickers/pens
- Group agreement
- Blu-Tack
- Music on phone
- Stretchy ring
- Homemade songs and games book
- Marshmallow video clip
- Handout
- Evaluation forms
- Certificates
- Cake/fruit to share
- Relaxation script

Welcome (Headspace and Containment)

Invite parents/carers and children to come and sit with you in a circle; make name badges together.

Welcome everyone and thank them for coming.

Sing the hello song. How did HHH go this week?

Group agreement (Headspace and Containment)

Thank everyone for helping to make this such a safe and respectful group.

Circle time (Headspace and Containment)

Repeat favourite songs and games. Give out home-made books of the group's favourites – parents, carers and children could help to make these.

Breathing and regulation (Regulation and Relaxation)

Practise together for a few minutes.

Watching and wondering (Head, Heart and Hands)

Play the "clay" game: Demonstrate this with your co-practitioner or a volunteer parent/carer first. Co-practitioner crouches on floor like a lump of clay, and you ask their permission to gently mould and move them into different shapes. The "clay" allows their partner to move them gently. All movements must abide by the group agreement – safety and respect. Parent/carer is the clay first, then swap with the child. During this exercise, invite parents/carers to really tune into their children's thoughts and feelings – "practise your HHH". No talking throughout game.

HINT: Quiet, gentle music playing on a phone or Bluetooth speaker.

Loving touch (Head, Heart and Hands)

Favourite story massage or games.

A "gift" or "Bag of Ideas": sharing ideas and information with parents and carers (Developmental knowledge)

Watch the Marshmallow Test video clip together.

Handout: Share with parents/carers the lovely information sheet on how helpful behaviour follows secure attachment (available online).

Reiterate the message that children with loving and sensitive relationships with their parents/carers behave better and do better – it might just need patience!

Creative relaxation (Regulation and Relaxation)

Enjoy together.

Try this at home (Head, Heart and Hands)

Ask parents to continue HHH at home every day.

Also ask them to have a "play date" with their child at least once a week – just one-on-one, with no phones or interruptions. This will make a huge difference to the quality of their relationship. They can play with the shoebox, or develop their own playtime ideas.

Brief recap and goodbyes (Headspace and Containment)

Just recap gently what we have covered over the past six weeks.

Evaluation

Presentation of certificates to all members

Cake and fruit to enjoy!

If possible, provide parents and carers with information on other groups and services which may support their relationships going forward.

Goodbyes.

Appendix 4

A programme for parents, carers and their children and teenagers

Six sample sessions for 10-to-14-year-olds*

* approximate age group

H2H 10 to 14 years: Week 1 "Welcome to H2H"

Welcome (Headspace and Containment)

Pop music or similar playing.

Invite parents/carers and teens to come and sit with you in a circle; make name badges.

Welcome everyone and thank them for coming.

Group agreement (Headspace and Containment)

Invite parents and children to help you write a short list of things that will help the group go well and be a safe place for all. Examples: mobiles on silent, respect everyone, listen to everyone, we are equal in this space, etc. Ensure that all group members have a voice in this exercise.

Circle time (Headspace and Containment)

Gently introduce the session structure; each week we begin with low-key activities. Our names: give everyone a sheet of paper and pens to make a poster all about them – their name and things they like, etc. If possible, laminate these, which makes them look great. If appropriate, practitioners can share their own posters first and then invite parents and children to share theirs – where their name comes from, what it means, things they like, etc. NB: volunteers only.

Breathing and regulation (Regulation and Relaxation)

"Build A High Tower" game.

Invite parent, carer and teen pairs to take some straws and build a tower together using just straws and tape. Make it as high as you can manage in ten minutes! No talking allowed. Admire the towers.

As an alternative, use empty toilet roll tubes or anything light, safe and cheap (and free). This game will encourage regulation, balance and breathing.

Watching and wondering (Head, Hearts and Hands)

Explain that research shows that parents who spend time really thinking about their children and teens begin to understand them. Better still, this can really help strengthen their relationship.

Play "Seeing the world through my eyes" game. Sit back-to-back on chairs with paper and pens. Parent/carer has a sheet with a simple drawing on it, e.g. a house, toy animal, laptop, birthday cake (adapt as needed for culture and context). They describe the picture to their child, who tries to draw what she is hearing – parent is not allowed to use the words "house", "home" or similar, but just describes shapes, lines and details, and where to draw them. Now swap over.

Now share the pictures with each other – how easy is it to make yourself understood? It's actually really hard to read someone's mind – but trying to do it can help us understand and feel understood.

HINT: Quiet, gentle music playing on a phone or Bluetooth speaker.

Loving touch (Head, Heart and Hands)

Invite parents and youngsters to sit in a circle all facing in one direction. Invite them to join in a fun story which we will tell on each other's backs! NB: Everyone must ask the person in front of them for permission to touch them – also remind everyone about our group agreement. Use the cooking massage story (script in online resource bank), or make up your own. Then all turn and do it in the other direction!

As an alternative, sit in a circle facing one way, ask for permission from the person in front and then draw their name on their back using your finger with a firm and gentle pressure. Then try asking them to "break the code" as a short message, e.g. "Hello" or a colour, is written on their back; the person in front must see if they can work out what the message is. Swap over. Emphasise that we are not trying to catch people out, but actually trying to help them to tune into our intentions.

A "gift" or "Bag of Ideas": sharing ideas and information with parents and carers (Developmental knowledge)

Each week, we share with the group a gift or an idea – something to nurture parents, carers and teens – and also share important information about the emotional development of older children and teenagers. Give out funny sheet about communication and listening (available online).

Creative relaxation (Regulation and Relaxation)

Explain that each week we enjoy a creative relaxation together; invite the group to join in and enjoy some peaceful and relaxing time (sample scripts in online resource bank). Play calm music in the background and read the story in a calm voice at a nice unhurried pace.

Try this at home (Head, Heart and Hands)

Ask parents, carers and teens to practise listening this week – just in case they are misunderstanding each other. Parents, try especially hard to put yourself in your youngster's shoes and see things from her point of view.

Brief recap of the session and see you next time (Headspace and Containment)

Just recap gently what we have covered today and thank parents and children for coming and taking the time out of their busy days. End with goodbyes and see you next week for our second session together. Play out with pop music or similar.

H2H 10 to 14 years: Week 2 "The amazing teenage brain"

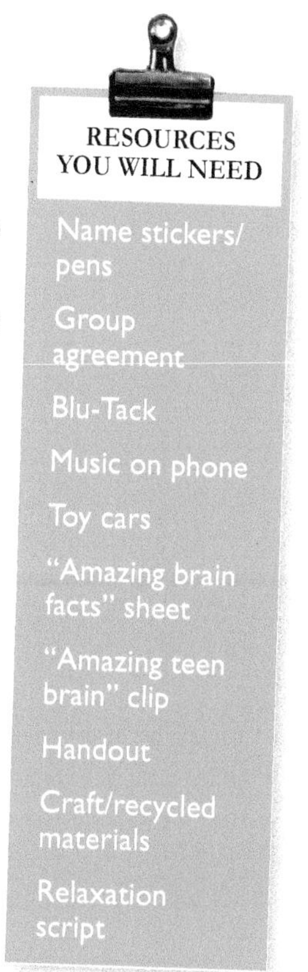

Welcome (Headspace and Containment)

Music on - circle – make name badges together.

Welcome everyone and thank them for coming.

Group agreement (Headspace and Containment)

Is this working OK? Anything to add?

Circle time (Headspace and Containment)

Going round the circle, we introduce ourselves: "My name is … and today my favourite animal is a …". Make it clear that people can "pass" if they want – no pressure, it's just lovely to get to know a bit more about each other and things we like.

Breathing and regulation (Regulation and Relaxation)

Give each parent/carer and teen pair a toy car and nothing else. Their challenge is to start at one side of the room and get the car to the other side without the tyres leaving the surface of anything. Three rules: (1) people can't walk holding the car, (2) the car is not allowed on the floor at any time and (3) the game is played in complete silence. They can use anything safe to hand as the "road", including themselves. It's not a race – it's about working together to do an excellent job! Make the challenge easier or harder as appropriate.

Watching and wondering (Head, Heart and Hands)

Invite parents, carers and teens to stand facing each other, feet apart, arms stretched out straight in front. Invite them to push their hands together, feel some gentle pushing pressure, and try to find a balance. Parents need to tune into their teen because the teenager decides when to move her feet back and the parent must be ready. Move feet back and try to balance again, and again. Parents, really tune in to your teen. Try with using only one arm each to balance. Have fun with this – it is a game of cooperation and mind-reading.

HINT: Quiet, gentle music playing on a phone or Bluetooth speaker.

NB: This is the start of us focusing on RF. We take slow steps, week by week.

Loving touch (Head, Heart and Hands)

Circle massage (ask permission). Use the weather story (available online).

A "gift" or "Bag of Ideas": sharing ideas and information with parents and carers (Developmental knowledge)

Introducing the "amazing teenage brain"– DVD clips (links online).

Offer each pair a selection of recycled boxes, card, craft materials, stickers, sequins, etc. and ask them to have fun building a model of a teenage brain. Take photos, which can be printed out even if the model can't be kept.

Handout and exercises: the amazing teenage brain – for parents/carers and teens.

Recommended (and hilarious!) book: Nicola Morgan's *Blame My Brain – The Amazing Teenage Brain Revealed* (www.nicolamorgan.com/books/blame-my-brain).

Creative relaxation (Regulation and Relaxation)

Enjoy together; if possible make music available for them to take home to practise – suggested music links online.

Try this at home (Head, Heart and Hands)

Ask parents, carers and teens to keep in mind that the teenage brain is an amazing thing and undergoing the most profound change since the age of two – maybe have a look at the "Amazing brain facts" sheet a few times. Gently hint that most parents have amnesia when it comes to remembering their own teenagehood! Of course, they tidied their rooms, did all their homework, said please and thank you in all the right places and never ever did anything like the teens of today do, did they? And teenagers never believe that their parents were actually young and cool once. How could that possibly be true? Actually, we all went through this very special time, and harnessing the power of the teenage brain can really maximise future chances and success.

Brief recap of the session and see you next time (Headspace and Containment)

Just recap gently what we have covered today and thank parents and children for coming and taking the time out of their busy days. Fun music to see group out. See you next week for session 3.

H2H 10 to 14 years: Week 3 "Things I like about you"

Welcome (Headspace and containment)

Music on – circle – make name badges together.

Welcome everyone and thank them for coming.

Group agreement (Headspace and Containment)

Is this working OK? Anything to add?

Circle time (Headspace and Containment)

Going round the circle, we introduce ourselves: "My name is … and today my favourite colour is …". Make it clear that people can "pass" if they want – no pressure, it's just lovely to get to know a bit more about each other.

Breathing and regulation (Regulation and Relaxation)

Today we are going to try some conducted breathing. Invite everyone to stand in the circle with feet apart and hands on their ribcage. Invite them to breathe in and out deeply; try and make your ribcage move in and out – nice deep breathing.

Now everyone breathe in for a count of 3, hold for 3 and breathe out for 3.

Repeat for 6, 9 and 12 – this is not a competition, it's just to remind us to take time to breathe deeply through the day, especially when we are stressed or feeling overwhelmed. Practise together for a few minutes.

Watching and wondering (Head, Heart and Hands)

Invite parents, carers and teens to stand facing each other, feet apart, arms stretched out straight in front. Invite them to hold each other's wrists firmly and gently.

This time the challenge is for both to sit down on the floor without falling or pulling each other over, and then stand up again – all without breaking hold! Parents really tune in to your teen. Try to mind-read when she will move and keep with her. This game is completed in silence.

HINT: Quiet, gentle music playing on a phone or Bluetooth speaker.

Loving touch (Head, Heart and Hands)

Musical instruments story massage as per cultural setting.

A "gift" or "Bag of Ideas": sharing ideas and information with parents and carers (Developmental knowledge)

Share the "Is it full?" story, using a cup filled with stones (script online). Acknowledge that we all have things we don't like very much about each other. – and we all have good reason. It's easy to focus on the negative things. The "Is it full?" story shows that there is always room for us to grow and improve, even when we are old.

Now invite everyone to think of one thing that they really appreciate about their parent/carer or teen – just something small. Give out small cards and take some time to make a "I really like ..." card with pens, stickers, etc. Be sensitive about whether it is appropriate for these to be given – maintain the privacy of each relationship.

Creative relaxation (Regulation and Relaxation)

Enjoy together – has anyone tried doing this at home?

Try this at home (Head, Heart and Hands)

Encourage all to focus on appreciating the things they like about each other, even though the negative may not have gone away. We've all got room to grow and change!

Brief recap of the session and see you next time (Headspace and Containment)

Just recap gently what we have covered today and thank parents and children for coming and taking the time out of their busy days. End with goodbyes and music out; see you next week for session 4.

H2H 10 to 14 years: Week 4 "heart-to-heart"

Welcome (Headspace and Containment)

Music on – circle – make name badges together.

Welcome everyone and thank them for coming.

Group agreement (Headspace and Containment)

Is this working OK? Anything to add?

Circle time (Headspace and Containment)

Going round the circle, we introduce ourselves: "My name is … and today something I would like to try is …". Make it clear that people can "pass" if they want – no pressure.

The "something" could be anything from a type of food to travelling somewhere new.

Breathing and regulation (Regulation and Relaxation)

Practise conducted breathing. Invite everyone to stand in the circle with feet apart and hands on their ribcage. Invite them to breathe in through the nose and out through the mouth; try and make your ribcage move out and back – nice deep breaths.

Now everyone breathe in for a count of 3, hold for 3 and breathe out for 3.

Repeat for 6, 9 and 12; this is not a competition, but just to remind us to take time to breathe deeply through the day, especially when we are stressed or feeling overwhelmed. If the group takes to this well, ask them to imagine that, as they breathe in, a golden thread is pulling them up towards the ceiling and that, as they breathe out, their feet are burrowing deep into the floor.

Watching and wondering (Head, Heart and Hands)

This is a grown-up version of musical statues, called "Hunters".

Teens stand at one end of the room and the parents/carers at the other end opposite them. Parents can move forward whilst their teen's back is turned but must freeze when they turn – just have fun with this. NB: Parent/carer is not out if they are seen moving. Swap over so that the parents are the hunters. Encourage relaxed play.

Next, invite teens to stand really still and parent/carer to stand opposite them (like a mirror reflection). The teenager can move subtly at any point and the parent must copy the move as quickly as possible – really small movements, like a look, tilt of the head, or flick of a finger. Parents have to tune in and try to imagine and predict what might come next. It should look like a perfect mirror reflection!

Ask parents/carers to tune into their youngster – what is she thinking and feeling; can I respond to her quickly and mirror her accurately?

The pair can now change who is in charge at any point – without speaking, they tune in to each other and alternate who is the mover and who is the reflection. The practitioner walks around the group trying to guess who is in charge – participants try to make it impossible for the practitioner to work it out.

Loving touch (Head, Heart and Hands)

"Packing a suitcase" massage story – first in one direction, then turn and do it the other way round!

A "gift" or "Bag of Ideas": sharing ideas and information with parents and carers (Developmental knowledge)

A small heart-shaped stone, crystal or card with a heart on – introduce the idea of attachment (ideas for suitable DVD clips available online).

Share heads, heart and hands and go through each carefully. Let parents know that they need to do this for their teenagers so that the latter can also learn to do it – share the idea of the transmission of attachment down the generations.

Read to the group the story *I'll Love You Forever* by Robert Munsch (http://robertmunsch.com/book/love-you-forever) to illustrate how the transmission of attachment works.

Creative relaxation (Regulation and Relaxation)

Enjoy together.

Try this at home (Head, Heart and Hands)

Ask parents/carers and teens to practise HHH: basically, practise your mind-reading on each other and try to let each other know that you understand them. Both can practise, but the grown-ups are responsible for this in the here-and-now. In the future, the youngsters will be this "kind and reflective mind" for any children they care for.

Brief recap of the session and see you next time (Headspace and Containment)

Just recap gently what we have covered today and thank parents and children for coming and taking the time out of their busy days. Pop music to see us out. Two more sessions left!

H2H 10 to 14 years: Week 5 "Choices and consequences"

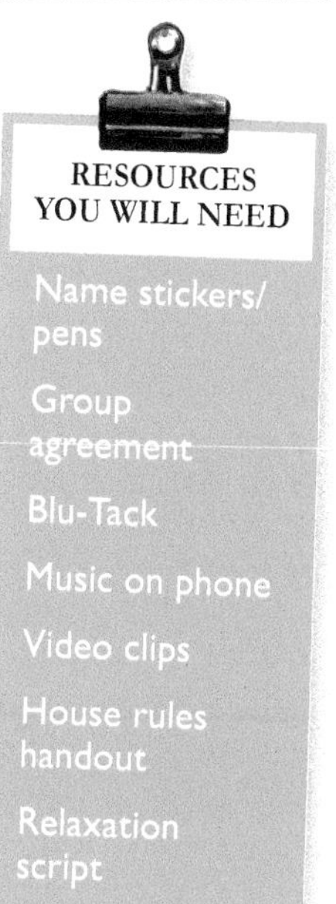

Welcome (Headspace and Containment)

Music on – circle – make name badges together.

Welcome everyone and thank them for coming.

Group agreement (Headspace and Containment)

Is this working OK? Anything to add?

Circle time (Headspace and Containment)

Going round the circle, we introduce ourselves: "My name is … and today something I would like to change about the world is …". Make it clear that people can "pass" if they want – no pressure.

Breathing and regulation (Regulation and Relaxation)

In our circle, just take a few deep breaths. Practitioner asks group to copy her first. Practitioner starts a simple clapping rhythm, for example three claps and a pause – keep it going for a little while, change it, then change it again. Now explain that anyone in the group can lead if they want to and we all have to tune in. Without speaking, someone else can take over and we all tune in and follow. We try to make the shifts from one to another as sensitively and seamlessly as possible.

Watching and wondering (Head, Heart and Hands)

Watch one of the suggested video clips together (e.g. "talking twins" clip – link online); ask parents and teenagers to guess what they think is going on – thoughts, feelings and actions. Refer back to HHH.

Next stage: ask everyone to notice that we weren't just guessing about the intentions of the twins – we also had our own feelings about what was happening. *Our* feelings are involved in our interactions in complicated ways – our thoughts and feelings affect how we feel about the other person. "Actually, it's me and you often getting in a muddle because my thoughts affect yours, then I have feelings about your thoughts, which affect your feelings – and before we know it, we are in a right old mess." (Just having a discussion about this can help parents/carers and youngsters become more aware and reflective about how they affect each other from moment to moment).

Loving touch (Head, Heart and Hands)

Favourite massage story, or invite parent/carer and teen to create their own family one.

A "gift" or "Bag of Ideas": sharing ideas and information with parents and carers (Developmental knowledge)

Research shows that when children and teenagers are involved in agreeing the house rules, they generally work quite well. It's a bit like our group agreement. Children and teens can also agree the consequences for breaking rules (information sheet in online resource bank).

Creative relaxation (Regulation and Relaxation)

Enjoy together.

Try this at home (Head, Heart and Hands)

Encourage everyone to practise HHH in the coming week.

Have a go at negotiating an agreement for the house rules.

Next week we can catch up and see how we got on.

Brief recap of the session and see you next time (Headspace and Containment)

Just recap gently what we have covered today and thank parents and children for coming and taking the time out of their busy days. Next week is our final week – cake and fruit to celebrate!

Pop music to see us out.

H2H 10 to 14 years: Week 6 "Celebrations"

Welcome (Headspace and Containment)

Music on – circle – make name badges together.

Welcome everyone and thank them for coming.

Group agreement (Headspace and Containment)

Thank everyone for helping to make this such a safe and supportive group.

Circle time (Headspace and Containment)

Going round the circle, we introduce ourselves: "My name is … and today something I would like to say about this group is …".

Breathing and regulation (Regulation and Relaxation)

In our circle, just take a few deep breaths

The ultimate counting game: practitioner explains that the challenge is to count from 1 to as high as the group can get without speaking at the same time. Anyone can start with 1, anyone else can add 2, 3 and so on, but if two people speak at once, you have to start again at 1! Have fun! This is the ultimate in tuning in and regulating, and can be played at home, in the car and other places.

Watching and wondering (Head, Heart and Hands)

Final practice of HHH.

Video clip(s). Watch together and keep pausing – ask parents, carers and teens to guess what is happening, what this person is thinking and feeling. How could we let them know that we understand it?

The group can also try to predict what they think is going to happen next. Watch, pause and discuss as the video plays. (There are lots of suggested YouTube clips in the online resource bank; there are some hilarious ones involving animals, which makes the guessing lots of fun.)

Loving touch (Head, Heart and Hands)

Favourite massage story or own family one.

A "gift" or "Bag of Ideas": sharing ideas and information with parents and carers (Developmental knowledge)

Doodles and scribbles – time to relax, with nice gentle music on in the background.

Give out small plain notebooks and bundles of pens to encourage us all to take time to doodle, relax and reflect. We hope you enjoy them – take time to look after *you*.

Creative relaxation (Regulation and Relaxation)

Enjoy together.

Try this at home (Head, Heart and Hands)

Encourage everyone to practise HHH. We will be amazed at the difference it makes to all of our relationships. Practise on each other, your teachers, your friends, your manager, your partner – RF skills improve relationships!

Brief recap and goodbyes (Headspace and Containment)

Just recap gently on what we have covered over the six weeks and thank parents, carers and teens for coming and taking the time out of their busy days.

Evaluation forms.

Present certificates to all.

Cake and fruit to enjoy together.

If appropriate, provide information for families about other support services.

Goodbyes.

Epilogue

This is dedicated to all those practitioners who, week after week and year after year, dedicate themselves to supporting parents and carers and their children.

I invite you to kick off your shoes, pull up a cosy chair in a quiet and undisturbed place and take the time to rest and reflect. Please put on some relaxing and calming music and take some lovely deep breaths.

I would like to encourage you to take time every day to make sure that you are OK and your batteries are recharged. The work you do is amazing!

Here is a small gift from me to you. I hope that you enjoy it!

"The tree of life"

Find a comfortable position and close your eyes; take a few minutes just for you to rest and feel refreshed.

Focus on your breathing and feel your lungs gently filling with breath and then the breath gently leaving your body – in and out – in your own gentle rhythm. If you can, breathe in through your nose so that the air is warm as it enters your lungs, and breathe out through your mouth.

Bring your attention to the top of your head and imagine that your scalp is tight and tense. Take a deep breath in, and as you breathe out let your scalp completely relax as if it is pulling downwards – smooth and heavy. Feel your head become nice and warm.

Bring your attention to your neck and again imagine that it is stiff and tense. Take a deep breath in, and as you breathe out feel your neck relax and that nice warm feeling trickle down from your head.

Bring your attention to your shoulders and imagine them hunched and tight. Breathe in deeply, and as you breathe out let your shoulders relax and gently pull downwards – feeling lovely and warm and relaxed.

Bring your attention to your body – to your stomach, lungs and heart and to each vertebra of your spine. Take a deep breath in, and as you breathe out feel your whole body become heavy and warm, relaxing into the chair as if you are sinking into a soft, fluffy cloud.

Imagine your legs growing heavier and heavier into the chair, and as you breathe in deeply feel your legs relax all the way down to your feet. Feel that lovely warm, calm feeling trickle down your legs and into your feet and out through the tips of your toes.

If you would like to listen to my words and follow me on a journey to a beautiful field of dreams, then please do so. If you would like to stay in this lovely calm place, then please do so – whatever you choose. You can open your eyes at any time if you feel you need to and it will bring you straight back to this room.

Imagine that you are standing barefoot on some delightful green grass that feels springy beneath your feet – the sun is shining and there is a gentle breeze on your cheeks. You are walking down a grassy path to a gate and as you open the gate you enter a lovely meadow – this is a safe and beautiful place, and only you can be here.

There are wild flowers growing around you and you can smell their gentle scent upon the air. Butterflies and bumblebees make their way from flower to flower and you can hear birds singing above. Your eyes are drawn to the middle of the field. An ancient tree stands before you – it has been here for hundreds of years. You clamber onto the lower branches of the tree and realise that, as you reach out to hold the thick trunk, it embraces you and you are taken into the fabric of the tree itself. You feel your ancient roots burrowing deep into the rich soil, deeper and deeper into the cool ground. Your roots keep you steady and seek out the water that sustains you. You feel your arms stretching upwards and becoming the willowy branches reaching for the sky. The branches are strong, and when you look closer you realise that there are creatures and birds, which find refuge in your arms. The winds might come to swirl around you but this tree is strong and its roots are deep. It has stood through many storms, and flourishes every springtime.

You gently step back out of the tree and take a glance backwards

– you take this glance with you as you walk back towards the gate that leads back from the field. You open the gate and step through, and tread back along the grassy path towards waking up.

10, 9, 8 – feel the ground beneath your feet and gently wiggle your fingers and toes

7, 6, 5 – you are preparing yourself to wake up very slowly and gently

4, 3, 2, 1 – open your eyes and gently stretch – give yourself a warm smile.

References

Aber, J.L., Slade, A., Berger, B., Bregsi, I. and Kaplan, M. (1985) *Parent Development Interview.* Unpublished manuscript. New York: Barnard College.

Ainsworth, M.D.S, Blehar, M.C., Waters, E. and Wall, S. (1978) *Patterns of Attachment: A psychological study of the Strange Situation.* Hillsdale, NJ: Lawrence Erlbaum Associates.

Allen, J.G., Fonagy, P. and Bateman, A.W. (2008) *Mentalizing in clinical practice.* Washington DC: American Psychiatric Publishing.

Andreassen, C. and West, J. (2007) Measuring socio-economic functioning in a national birth cohort study. *Infant Mental Health Journal*, 28(6): 627–46.

Arnott, B. and Meins, E. (2007) Links between antenatal attachment representations, postnatal mind-mindedness, and infant attachment security: A preliminary study of mothers and fathers. *Bulletin of the Menninger Clinic*, 71(2): 132–49.

Bammens, S., Adkins, T. and Badger, J. (2015) Psycho-educational intervention increases reflective functioning in foster and adoptive parents. *Adoption and Fostering*, 39(1): 38–50.

Baradon, T., Fonagy, P., Bland, K., Lenard, K. and Sleed, M. (2008) New Beginnings – an experience-based programme addressing the attachment relationship between mothers and their babies in prisons. *Journal of Child Psychotherapy*, 34(2): 240–58.

Barlow, J. (2016) Improving relationships in the perinatal period: what works? *Association of Infant Mental Health and International Journal of Birth and Parent Education Best Practice Guidelines*, No.1, Spring.

Baron-Cohen, S., Tager-Flusberg, H. and Cohen, D.J. (1993) *Understanding other minds: Perspectives from autism.* Oxford: Oxford University Press.

Baskett, L.M. and Johnson, S.M. (1982) The young child's interactions with parents versus siblings: A behavioural analysis. *Child Development*, 53(3): 643–50.

Belsky, J., Fish, M. and Isabella, R. (1991) Continuity and discontinuity in infant negative and positive emotionality: Family antecedents and attachment consequences. *Developmental Psychology*, 27(3): 421–31.

Berlin, L.J. and Cassidy, J. (2003) Mothers' self-reported control of their preschool children's emotional expressiveness: A longitudinal study of associations with infant-mother attachment and children's emotional regulation. *Social Development*, 12(4): 477–95.

Bjelland, I., Dahl, A.A., Haug, T.T. and Neckelmann, D. (2002) The validity of the Hospital Anxiety and Depression Scale: An updated literature review. *Journal of Psychosomatic Research*, 52(2): 69–77.

Bornstein, M.H. and Manian, N. (2013) Maternal responsiveness and sensitivity re-considered: some is more. *Developmental Psychopathology*, 25(4 Pt 1): 957–71.

Bowlby, J. (1969) *Attachment and Loss I: Attachment*. New York: Basic Books.

Brandon, A.R., Pitts, S., Denton, W.H., Stringer, C.A and Evans, H.M. (2009) A history of the theory of prenatal attachment. *Journal of Prenatal and Perinatal Psychological Health*, 23(4): 201–22.

Brown, F. (2012) The play behaviours of Roma children in Transylvania. *International Journal of Play*, 1(1): 64–74.

Brown, F. and Webb, S. (2005) Children without play. *Journal of Education*, 35: 139–58.

Bruce, T. (2011) *Cultivating creativity for babies, toddlers and young children*. London: Hodder.

Carlson, V., Cicchetti, D., Barnett, D., and Braunwald, K. (1989) Disorganized/disoriented attachment relationships in maltreated infants. *Developmental Psychology*, 25(4): 525–31.

Choi-Kain, L.W. and Gunderson, J.G. (2008) Mentalization: Ontogeny, assessment, and application in the treatment of borderline personality disorder. *American Journal of Psychiatry*, 165(9): 1127–35.

Cohen, N., Muir, E., Lojkasek, M., Muir, R., Parker, C., Barwick,

M. and Brown, M. (1999) Watch, wait and wonder: Testing the effectiveness of a new approach to mother-infant psychotherapy. *Infant Mental Health Journal*, 20(4): 429–51.

Condon, J.T. (1993) The assessment of antenatal emotional attachment: Development of a questionnaire instrument. *British Journal of Medical Psychology*, 66 (Pt 2): 167–83.

Condon, J. and Corkingdale, C. (1998) The assessment of parent-to-infant attachment: development of a self-report questionnaire instrument. *Journal of Reproductive and Infant Psychology*, 16: 57–76.

Cooper, P.J., Tomlinson, M., Swartz, L., Landman, M., Molteno, C., Stein, A., McPherson, K. and Murray, L. (2009) Improving quality of mother-infant relationship and infant attachment in socioeconomically deprived community in South Africa: Randomised controlled trial. *British Medical Journal*, 338: b974 doi:10.1136/bmj.b974.

Cox, J.L., Holden, J.M. and Sagovsky, R. (1987) Detection of postnatal depression: development of the 10-item Edinburgh postnatal depression scale. *British Journal of Psychiatry*, 150(6): 782–86.

Crnic, K. and Booth, C.L. (1991) Hassles of parenting across early childhood. *Journal of Marriage and Family*, 53(4): 1042–50.

De Wolff, M.S. and van Ijzendoorn, M.H. (1997) Sensitivity and attachment. A meta-analysis on parental antecedents of infant attachment. *Child Development*, 68(4): 571–91.

Dozier, M., Manni, M. and Lindheim, O. (2005) Lessons from the longitudinal studies of attachment. In K.E. Grossman, K. Grossman and E. Waters (eds.) *Attachment from infancy to adulthood: The major longitudinal studies*. New York: The Guilford Press.

Dozier, M., Stovali, K. and Albus, K. (1999) Attachment and psychopathology in adulthood. In J. Cassidy and P. Shaver (eds.) *Handbook of Attachment: Theory, Research and Clinical Applications*. New York: Guilford.

Egeland, B. and Carlson, E. (2004) Attachment and psychopathology. In L. Atkinson and S. Goldberg (eds.) *Attachment issues in psychopathology and intervention*. Hillsdale, NJ: Lawrence Erlbaum Associates.

Feldman, R., Gordon, I. and Zagoory-Sharon, O. (2010) The cross-generation transmission of oxytocin in humans. *Hormones and Behavior*, 58(4): 669–76.

Fonagy, P., Gergely, G., Jurist, E.L. and Target, M. (2004) *Affect regulation, mentalization and the development of the self*. London: Karnac Books.

Fonagy, P., Leigh, T. and Steele, M. (1996). The relation of attachment status, psychiatric classification and response to psychotherapy. *Journal of Consulting and Clinical Psychology*, 64(1): 22–31.

Fonagy, P. and Levinson, A. (2004) Offending and attachment: The relationship between interpersonal awareness and offending in a prison population with psychiatric disorder. *Canadian Journal of Psychoanalysis*, 12(2): 225–51.

Fonagy, P., Steele, H. and Steele, M. (1991) Maternal representations of attachment during pregnancy predict the organization of infant-mother attachment at one year of age. *Child Development*, 62(5): 891–905.

Fonagy, P., Steele, H., Moran, G., Steele, M. and Higgitt, A. (1991). The capacity for understanding mental states: The reflective self in parent and child and its significance for security of attachment. *Infant Mental Health Journal*,12(3): 201–18.

Fonagy, P. and Target, M. (1997) Attachment and reflective function: Their role in self-organization. *Development and Psychopathology*, 9(4): 679–700.

Fraiberg, S., Adelson, E. and Shapiro, V. (1975) Ghosts in the nursery: A psychoanalytic approach to the problems of impaired infant–mother relationships. *Journal of American Academy for Child and Adolescent Psychiatry*, 14(3): 387–421.

Goldberg, S. (2000) *Attachment and development*. London: Arnold.

Goodman, R. (1997) The Strengths and Difficulties Questionnaire: A Research Note. *Journal of Child Psychology and Psychiatry*, 38(5): 581–6.

Goodman, R., Meltzer, H. and Bailey, V. (1998) The Strengths and Difficulties Questionnaire: A pilot study on the validity of the self-report version. *European Child and Adolescent Psychiatry*, 7(3): 125–30.

Gopnik, A. (1993) How we know our minds: The illusion of

first-person knowledge of intentionality. *Behavioural and Brain Sciences*, 16(1): 1–14.

Gopnik, A. (2009) *The philosophical baby: What children's minds tell us about truth, love and the meaning of life.* New York: Farrer, Strauss and Giroux.

Green, J. and Goldwyn, R. (2002) Annotation: Attachment disorganisation and psychopathology: new findings in attachment research and their potential implications for developmental psychopathology in childhood. *Journal of Child Psychology and Psychiatry*, 43(7): 835–46. doi: 10.1111/1469-7610.00102.

Greenberg, M. (1999) Attachment and psychopathology in childhood. In J. Cassidy and P. Shaver (eds.) *Handbook of Attachment: Theory, Research and Clinical Applications.* New York: Guilford Press.

Grienenberger, J., Kelly, K. and Slade, A. (2005) Maternal reflective functioning, mother-infant affective communication, and infant attachment: Exploring the link between mental states and observed caregiving behavior in the intergenerational transmission of attachment. *Attachment and Human Development*, 7(3): 299–311.

Harter, S. (1999) *The construction of the self: A developmental perspective.* New York: The Guilford Press.

Kalland, M., Fagerlund, A., von Koskull, M. and Pajulo, M. (2016) Families First: the development of a new mentalization-based group intervention for first-time parents to promote child development and family health. *Primary Health Care Research and Development*, 17(1): 3–17.

Katznelson, H. (2014) Reflective Functioning: A review. *Clinical Psychology Review*, 34(2): 107–17.

Kearney, J. and Cushing, E. (2012) A multi-modal pilot intervention with violence-exposed mothers in a child treatment program. *Issues in Mental Health Nursing*, 33(8): 544–52.

Kendall S. and Bloomfield L. (2005) Developing and validating, a tool to measure parenting self-efficacy. *Journal of Advanced Nursing*, 51(2): 174–81.

Laranjo, J., Bernier, A. and Meins, E. (2008) Associations between maternal mind-mindedness and infant attachment security:

Investigating the mediating role of maternal sensitivity. *Infant Behavior and Development*, 31(4): 688–95.

Lester, S. and Russell, W. (2008) *Play for Change – Play, policy and Practice: A review of contemporary perspectives*. London: National Children's Bureau for Play for England.

Ma, K. (2006) Attachment theory in adult psychiatry. Part 1: Conceptualisations, measurement and clinical research findings. *Advances in Psychiatric Treatment*, 12(6): 440–49.

Main, M. (1994) A move to the level of representation in the study of attachment organization: Implications for psychoanalysis. *Bulletin of the British Psycho-Analytical Society* 1–15.

Main, M. and Solomon, J. (1986) Discovery of a new, insecure-disorganized/disoriented attachment pattern. In T.B. Brazelton and M. Yogman (eds.) *Affective development in infancy*. Norwood, New Jersey: Ablex.

Main, M. and Solomon, J. (1990) Procedures for identifying disorganized/disoriented infants during the Ainsworth Strange Situation. In M. Greenberg, D. Cicchetti and M. Cummings (eds.) *Attachment in the preschool years*. Chicago: University of Chicago Press.

Maskell-Graham, D. (2009) *Baby Bonding: An evaluation of the effect of lullaby and movement practices on maternal behaviours associated with attachment*. Unpublished thesis. Canterbury Christ Church University.

McDonough, S.C. (2004) Interaction Guidance: Promoting and nurturing the caregiving relationship. In A. Sameroff, S.C. McDonough and K.L. Rosenblum (eds.) *Treating parent-infant relationship problems: Strategies for intervention*. New York: Guilford Press.

Meins, E., Fernyhough, C., de Rosnay, M., Arnott, B., Leekam, S.R. and Turner, M. (2012) Mind-mindedness as a multidimensional construct: Appropriate and non-attuned mind-related comments independently predict infant–mother attachment in a socially diverse sample. *Infancy*, 17(4): 393–415.

Meins, E., Fernyhough, C., Fradley, E. and Tuckey, M. (2001) Rethinking maternal sensitivity: Mothers' comments on infants' mental processes predict security of attachment at 12 months. *Journal of Child Psychology and Psychiatry*, 42(5): 637–48.

Meins, E., Fernyhough, C., Wainwright, R., Clark-Carter, D., Das Gupta, M., Fradley, E. and Tuckey, M. (2003) Pathways to understanding mind: Construct validity and predictive validity of maternal mind-mindedness. *Child Development*, 74(4): 1194–211.

Meins, E., Fernyhough, C., Wainwright, R., Das Gupta, M., Fradley, E. and Tuckey, M. (2002) Maternal mind-mindedness and attachment security as predictors of theory of mind understanding. *Child Development*, 73(6): 1715–26.

Miller, A. (1987) *The Drama of Being a Child – The Search for the True Self*. London, UK: Virago Press.

Moutsiana, C., Fearon, P., Murray, L., Cooper, P., Goodyer, I., Johnstone, T. and Halligan, S. (2014) Making an effort to feel positive: insecure attachment in infancy predicts the neural underpinnings of emotion regulation in adulthood. *Journal of Child Psychology and Psychiatry*, 55(9): 999–1008.

Murray, L. (2000) *The Social Baby*. London: The Children's Project.

Oates, J.M. and Gervai, J. (2003) *Mothers' Object Relations Scale*. Poster presented at XI European Conference on Developmental Psychology. Milan, Italy.

O'Connor, T.G. and Croft, C.M. (2001) A twin study of attachment in preschool children. *Child Development*, 72(5): 1501–11.

Pajulo, M., Kalland, M., Sinkkonen, J., Helenius, H., Punamaki, R. and Suchman, N. (2012) Substance-abusing mothers in residential treatment with their babies: Importance of pre- and postnatal maternal Reflective Functioning. *Infant Mental Health Journal*, 33(1): 70–81.

Pajulo, M., Suchman, N., Kalland, M. and Mayes, L. (2006) Enhancing the effectiveness of residential treatment for substance abusing pregnant and parenting women: Focus on maternal reflective functioning and mother-child relationship. *Infant Mental Health Journal*, 33(1): 70–81.

Pawson, R. and Tilley, N. (1997) *Realistic Evaluation*. London: SAGE.

Pietromonaco, P.R. and Barrett, L.F. (2000) The internal working models concept: What do we really know about the self in relation to others? *Review of General Psychology*, 4(2): 155–75.

Rackett, P. and Holmes, B.M. (2010) Enhancing the attachment relationship: A prenatal perspective. *Educational and Child Psychology*, 27(3): 33–50.

Ravel, V., Goldberg, S., Atkinson, L., Benoit, D., Myhal, N., Poulton, L. and Zweirs, M. (2001) Maternal attachment, maternal responsiveness and infant attachment. *Infant Behavior and Development*, 24(3): 281–304.

Rispoli, K.M., McGoey, K.E., Kozid, N.A. and Schreiber, J.B. (2013) The relation of parenting, child temperament and attachment security in early childhood to social competence at school entry. *Journal of School Psychology*, 51(5): 643–58.

Sadler, L.S., Slade, A. and Mayes, L. (2006) Minding the Baby: A Mentalization based parenting program. In J. Allen and P. Fonagy (Eds.) *Handbook of Mentalization Based Treatment.* Chichester, UK: Wiley.

Schechter, D.S., Myers, M.M., Brunelli, S.A. and Coates, S.W. (2006) Traumatized mothers can change their minds about their toddlers: Understanding how a novel use of videofeedback supports positive change of maternal attributions. *Infant Mental Health Journal*, 27(5): 429–47.

Shai, D. (2010) Introducing parental embodied mentalising: Exploring moments of meeting of mind of parent and infants from a relational whole-body kinaesthetic perspective. In S. Bender (Ed.) *Movement analysis of interaction* (pp. 107–24). Berlin: Logos Verlag.

Shai, D. and Belsky, J. (2011) When words just won't do: Introducing Parental Embodied Mentalizing. *Child Development Perspectives*, 5(3): 173–80

Sharp, C. and Fonagy, P. (2008) The parent's capacity to treat the child as a psychological agent: Constructs, measures and implications for developmental psychopathology. *Social Development*, 17(3): 737–54.

Simkiss, D.E., MacCallum, F., Fan, E.E.Y., Oates, J.M., Kimani, P.K. and Stewart-Brown, S. (2013) Validation of the mothers object relations scales in 2–4 year old children and comparison with the child–parent relationship scale. *Health and Quality of Life Outcomes*, 11: 49.

Slade, A. (2005) Parental Reflective Functioning: An Introduction. *Attachment and Human Development*, 7(3): 269–82.

Slade, A. (2006) Reflective Parenting Programs: Theory and Development. *Psychoanalytic Inquiry*, 26(4): 640–57.

Slade, A., Bernbach, E., Grienenberger, J., Levy, D. and Locker, A. (2005) *Addendum to Fonagy, Target, Steele, and Steele reflective functioning scoring manual for use with the Parent Development Interview, Version 2.0.* Unpublished Manuscript. New York, NY: The City College and Graduate Center of the City University of New York.

Slade, A., Bernbach, E., Grienenberger, J., Levy, D.W. and Locker, A. (2002, 2005) *The parent development interview and The pregnancy interview.* Manual for scoring. New Haven, CT: Yale Child Study Center.

Slade, A., Grienenberger, J., Bernbach, E., Levy, D. and Locker, A. (2005) Maternal reflective functioning, attachment, and the transmission gap: A preliminary study. *Attachment and Human Development*, 7(3): 283–98.

Sleed, M., Baradon, T. and Fonagy, P. (2013) New Beginnings for mother and babies in prison: A cluster randomised controlled trial. *Attachment and Human Development*, 15(4): 349–67.

Söderström, K. and Skårderud, F. (2009) Minding the Baby. Mentalisation-based treatment in families with parental substance use disorder: Theoretical framework. *Nordic Psychology*, 61(3): 47–65.

Stern, D.N. (1985) *The interpersonal world of the infant: A view from psychoanalysis and developmental psychology.* New York: Basic Books.

Stern, T. (2014) The development of Reflective Functioning in a mother traumatised by past and present events: Facilitating change in the parent-infant relationship. *Journal of Infant, Child, and Adolescent Psychotherapy*, 13(1): 24–36.

Suchman, N.E., Decoste, C., Leigh, D. and Borelli, J. (2010) Reflective Functioning in mothers with drug use disorders: Implications for dyadic interactions with infants and toddlers. *Attachment and Human Development*, 12(6): 567–85.

Suess, G., Grossman, K. and Sroufe, A. (1992) Effects of infant attachment to mother and father on quality of adaptation in preschool: from dyadic to individual organization of self. *International Journal of Behavioral Development*, 15(1): 43–65.

Sutton-Smith, B. (1997) *The ambiguity of play*. Cambridge, MA: Harvard University Press.

Tomlin, A., Strum, L. and Kock, S. (2009) Observe, listen, wonder, and respond: A preliminary exploration of reflective function skills in early child care providers. *Infant Mental Health Journal*, 30(6): 634–47.

Tuckman, Bruce W. (1965) Developmental sequence in small groups. *Psychological Bulletin*, 63(6): 384–99.

Tuckman, Bruce W. and Jensen, M.A.C. (1977) Stages of small group development revisited. *Group and Organizational Studies*, 2(4): 419–27.

UNICEF (1991) *United Nations Convention on the Rights of the Child.* Stockholm: Svenska UNICEF Kommittén.

UNCRC (2013) *General comment No.17 (2013) on the right of the child to rest, leisure, play, recreational activities, cultural life and the arts (art. 31)*. CRC/C/GC/17. United Nations Committee on the Rights of the Child.

van Ijzendoorn, M.H., Schuengel, C. and Bakermans-Kranenburg, M.J. (1999) Disorganized attachment in early childhood: Meta-analysis of precursors, concomitants, and sequelae. *Development and Psychopathology*, 11(2): 225–49.

Weinfeld, N., Whaley, G., Egeland, B. and Carlson, E. (1999) The nature of individual differences in infant-caregiver attachment. In J. Cassidy and P. Shaver (eds.) *Handbook of Attachment: Theory, Research, and Clinical Applications*. New York: Guilford Press.

World Health Organization (2004) *The importance of caregiver–child interactions for the survival and healthy development of young children: A review*. Department of Child and Adolescent Health and Development.

Zigmond, A.S. and Snaith, R.P. (1983) The hospital anxiety and depression scale. *Acta Psychiatrica Scandinavica*, 67(6): 361–370.